Essentials of Latin Grammar

a practical guide
to the mastery of Latin

W. Michael Wilson

PASSPORT BOOKS
NTC/Contemporary Publishing Company

Titles Available in This Series:

Essentials of English Grammar
Essentials of Hindi Grammar
Essentials of Latin Grammar
Essentials of Russian Grammar
Essentials of Swedish Grammar
French Verbs and Essentials of Grammar
German Verbs and Essentials of Grammar
Italian Verbs and Essentials of Grammar
Japanese Verbs and Essentials of Grammar
Spanish Verbs and Essentials of Grammar

ISBN: 0-8442-8540-4

Published by Passport Books,
a division of NTC/Contemporary Publishing Group, Inc.
4255 West Touhy Avenue,
Lincolnwood (Chicago), Illinois 60646-1975 U.S.A.

Manufactured in the United States of America.

8 9 0 ML 9 8 7

Contents

ADDITIONAL SYNTAX

Preface

Essentials of Latin Grammar presents to its users the major grammatical concepts of the Latin language. The book is divided into two parts. In Part I, the primary emphasis is placed on *accidence,* the system of endings (or *inflections)* in Latin that express gender, number, tense, person, mood, or voice. Chapters in this section are first divided by parts of speech; then, two separate chapters treat numbers and dates. Part I, thus, provides users with a convenient reference to appropriate endings and rules of inflection—all of which are crucial to correct writing and perceptive reading in Latin. Part II of this book offers concise explanations of *syntax* (the use and interconnection of grammatical elements). The essential parts of Latin grammar are outlined in this section—from the function of noun cases to the numerous subordinate constructions that lend color and expression to writing in Latin. Part II concludes with a table of over 350 irregular verbs and their principal parts.

Examples illustrating grammar concepts were chosen for their authenticity—to represent the structures most frequently encountered in Roman literature. Each topic is treated separately, so that users of the book can either work on one topic at a time *or* quickly find the reference needed to help solve a particular difficulty. The synopsis of verb forms in the indicative and subjunctive moods, as well as in the active and passive voices, should prove an especially valuable reference tool. The abundant tables provide ample material both for creative exercises and for extended writing.

Essentials of Latin Grammar is a thorough handbook that lends itself to a variety of uses. Because its basic approach is to provide simple, concise explanations, it can be used by students of all levels—from those who have completed one semester's work to those who have attained a high level of mastery but who, from time to time, need a convenient reference to consult on difficult points of grammar. This book can be used for study and review, for individual or group work, as part of a refresher course or for research. The commanding importance of Latin in the development of Western Civilization also enhances the cultural significance of a thorough knowledge of the language.

Essentials of Latin Grammar is a unique and effective language-learning tool. Its author and the editors of Passport Books are confident that this comprehensive reference will prove indispensable to all those teaching and studying Latin.

Essential Accidence

I. NOUNS

1. Latin Nouns are divided into five groups called **Declensions.** Most nouns have **six** cases denoted by varied endings.

2. FIRST DECLENSION
All Nouns of the First Declension end in –**a** in the Nominative Singular.

rēgīna – rēgīnae (f), *queen.*

	SINGULAR	PLURAL
Nom.	rēgīn**a**	rēgīn**ae**
Voc.	rēgīn**a**	rēgīn**ae**
Acc.	rēgīn**am**	rēgīn**ās**
Gen.	rēgīn**ae**	rēgīn**ārum**
Dat.	rēgīn**ae**	rēgīn**īs**
Abl.	rēgīn**ā**	rēgīn**īs**

3. **Dea,** *goddess* and **fīlia**, *daughter* have their Dative and Ablative Plural, deā**bus** and fīliā**bus.**

4. Most Nouns of the First Declension are **Feminine** except, **poēta**, *poet*, **agricola,** *farmer*, **nauta**, *sailor* and **scrība,** *clerk* which are **Masculine.**

5. Second Declension

Masculine Nouns of the Second Declension end in **–us** in the Nominative Singular, apart from a few ending in **–er** or **–r.** Neuter Nouns of the Second Declension end in **–um.**

servus – servī (m), *slave.* **ager – agrī** (m), *field.*

	SINGULAR	PLURAL	SINGULAR	PLURAL
Nom.	serv**us**	serv**ī**	ag**er**	agr**ī**
Voc.	serv**e**	serv**ī**	ag**er**	agr**ī**
Acc.	serv**um**	serv**ōs**	agr**um**	agr**ōs**
Gen.	serv**ī**	serv**ōrum**	agr**ī**	agr**ōrum**
Dat.	serv**ō**	serv**īs**	agr**ō**	agr**īs**
Abl.	serv**ō**	serv**īs**	agr**ō**	agr**īs**

puer – puerī (m), *boy.* **vir – virī** (m), *man.*

	SINGULAR	PLURAL	SINGULAR	PLURAL
Nom.	pu**er**	puer**ī**	v**ir**	vir**ī**
Voc.	pu**er**	puer**ī**	v**ir**	vir**ī**
Acc.	puer**um**	puer**ōs**	vir**um**	vir**ōs**
Gen.	puer**ī**	puer**ōrum**	vir**ī**	vir**ōrum**
Dat.	puer**ō**	puer**īs**	vir**ō**	vir**īs**
Abl.	puer**ō**	puer**īs**	vir**ō**	vir**īs**

bellum – bellī (n), *war.* **deus – deī** (m), *god.*

	SINGULAR	PLURAL	SINGULAR	PLURAL
Nom.	bell**um**	bell**a**	de**us**	d**ī** (de**ī**)
Voc.	bell**um**	bell**a**	de**us**	d**ī** (de**ī**)
Acc.	bell**um**	bell**a**	de**um**	de**ōs**
Gen.	bell**ī**	bell**ōrum**	de**ī**	de**ōrum** (de**um**)
Dat.	bell**ō**	bell**īs**	de**ō**	d**īs** (de**īs**)
Abl.	bell**ō**	bell**īs**	de**ō**	d**īs** (de**īs**)

6. (*a*) **Fīlius**, *son* and **Proper** names ending in **–ius**, such as **Cornēlius, Pompēius** have their Vocative Singular in **–ī.**

e.g. **fīlī,** Cornēlī, Pompeī

(*b*) **Meus-a-um,** *my, mine,* has its Vocative Masculine Singular **mī.**

7. THIRD DECLENSION

The Third Declension is by far the biggest group of Nouns. They may be divided into **Five** groups (i) **Increasing** (ii) **Non-increasing** (iii) **Family Group** (iv) **Monosyllabics with stems ending in two consonants** (v) **Neuters ending in -ĕ, -al, -ar.** All genders are found.

N.B. The stem is found by taking the **Genitive Singular** and cutting off the ending, e.g. legiō, Genitive Singular legiō**nis** has the stem **legiōn–**

8. *Increasing Nouns*

A Noun is said to increase when it has **more** syllables in its **Genitive Singular** than in its **Nominative Singular.** An Increasing Noun has its Genitive Plural in –**um.**

mīles – mīlitis (m), *soldier.* **statiō – statiōnis** (f), *outpost.*

	SINGULAR	PLURAL	SINGULAR	PLURAL
Nom.	mīl**es**	mīlit**ēs**	stati**ō**	statiōn**ēs**
Voc.	mīl**es**	mīlit**ēs**	stati**ō**	statiōn**ēs**
Acc.	mīlit**em**	mīlit**ēs**	statiōn**em**	statiōn**ēs**
Gen.	mīlit**is**	mīlit**um**	statiōn**is**	statiōn**ūm**
Dat.	mīlit**ī**	mīlit**ibus**	statiōn**ī**	statiōn**ibus**
Abl.	mīlit**e**	mīlit**ibus**	statiōn**e**	statiōn**ibus**

flūmen – flūminis (n), *river.* **opus – operis** (n), *job, task.*

	SINGULAR	PLURAL	SINGULAR	PLURAL
Nom.	flūm**en**	flūmin**a**	op**us**	oper**a**
Voc.	flūm**en**	flūmin**a**	op**us**	oper**a**
Acc.	flūm**en**	flūmin**a**	op**us**	oper**a**
Gen.	flūmin**is**	flūmin**um**	oper**is**	oper**um**
Dat.	flūmin**ī**	flūmin**ibus**	oper**ī**	oper**ibus**
Abl.	flūmin**e**	flūmin**ibus**	oper**e**	oper**ibus**

9. *Non-Increasing Nouns*

A Non-Increasing Noun has the **same** number of syllables in its **Genitive Singular** as in its **Nominative Singular**. A Non-Increasing Noun has its Genitive Plural in –**ium.**

	hostis – hostis (m), *enemy.*		**nāvis – nāvis** (f), *ship.*	
	SINGULAR	PLURAL	SINGULAR	PLURAL
Nom.	host**is**	host**ēs**	nāv**is**	nāv**ēs**
Voc.	host**is**	host**ēs**	nāv**is**	nāv**ēs**
Acc.	host**em**	host**ēs**	nāv**em**	nāv**ēs**
Gen.	host**is**	host**ium**	nāv**is**	nāv**ium**
Dat.	host**ī**	host**ibus**	nāv**ī**	nāv**ibus**
Abl.	host**e**	host**ibus**	nāv**e**	nāv**ibus**

10. *Family Group*

The Family Group consists of **six** Nouns which are Non-Increasing but have their Genitive Plural in **–um.**

pater	**– patris**	(m),	*father*
māter	**– mātris**	(f),	*mother*
frāter	**– frātris**	(m),	*brother*
senex	**– senis**	(m),	*old man*
iuvenis	**– iuvenis**	(m),	*young man*
canis	**– canis**	(m),	*dog.*

11. *Monosyllabic Nouns*

Monosyllabic Nouns (i.e. Nouns of **one** syllable in the Nominative Singular) whose stem ends in **two consonants** have their Genitive Plural in **–ium.**

e.g.	**nox**	**– noctis**	(f),	*night*
	mōns	**– montis**	(m),	*mountain*
	pōns	**– pontis**	(m),	*bridge*
	fōns	**– fontis**	(m),	*fountain*
	gēns	**– gentis**	(f),	*tribe*
	urbs	**– urbis**	(f),	*city*
	dēns	**– dentis**	(m),	*tooth*
	os	**– ossis**	(n),	*bone*
	as	**– assis**	(n),	*as* (a Roman coin)
	arx	**– arcis**	(f),	*citadel*

12. *Neuter Nouns*

Neuter Nouns ending in **–ĕ, –al, –ar** decline as follows.

animal – animālis (n), *animal.* **mare – maris** (n), *sea.*

	SINGULAR	PLURAL	SINGULAR	PLURAL
Nom.	anim**al**	animāl**ia**	mar**e**	mar**ia**
Voc.	anim**al**	animāl**ia**	mar**e**	mar**ia**
Acc.	anim**al**	animāl**ia**	mar**e**	mar**ia**
Gen.	animāl**is**	animāl**ium**	mar**is**	—
Dat.	animāl**ī**	animāl**ibus**	mar**ī**	mar**ibus**
Abl.	animāl**ī**	animāl**ibus**	mar**ī**	mar**ibus**

also **cubīle – cubīlis** (n), *bed* and **calcar – calcāris** (n), *spur*

13. The following Nouns are irregular in declension.

vīs (f), *force* (in pl., *strength*). **bōs – bovis** (m), *ox.*

	SINGULAR	PLURAL	SINGULAR	PLURAL
Nom.	vīs	vīr**ēs**	bōs	bov**ēs**
Voc.	vīs	vīr**ēs**	bōs	bov**ēs**
Acc.	vi**m**	vīr**ēs**	bov**em**	bov**ēs**
Gen.	—	vīr**ium**	bov**is**	bo**um**
Dat.	—	vīr**ibus**	bov**ī**	bō**bus** (bu**bus**)
Abl.	v**ī**	vīr**ibus**	bov**e**	bō**bus** (bu**bus**)

Iuppiter – Iovis (m), *Jupiter.*

Nom.	Iuppit**er**	Gen.	Iov**is**
Voc.	Iuppit**er**	Dat.	Iov**ī**
Acc.	Iov**em**	Abl.	Iov**e**

14. Fourth Declension

Fourth Declension Nouns end in **–us** in the Nominative Singular and are mostly **Masculine.** There are two common **Neuter** Nouns which end in **–u** in the Nominative Singular, **genū-ūs**, *knee* and **cornu-ūs**, *horn, wing of an army.*

magistrātus – magistrātūs (m), *magistrate.*
genū – genūs (n), *knee.*

	SINGULAR	PLURAL	SINGULAR	PLURAL
Nom.	magistrāt**us**	magistrāt**ūs**	gen**ū**	gen**ua**
Voc.	magistrāt**us**	magistrāt**ūs**	gen**ū**	gen**ua**
Acc.	magistrāt**um**	magistrāt**ūs**	gen**ū**	gen**ua**
Gen.	magistrāt**ūs**	magistrāt**uum**	gen**ūs**	gen**uum**
Dat.	magistrāt**uī**	magistrāt**ibus**	gen**ū**	gen**ibus**
Abl.	magistrāt**ū**	magistrāt**ibus**	gen**ū**	gen**ibus**

15. There are a few Feminine Nouns, the commonest of which are, **manus-ūs** (f), *hand*, and **domus-ūs** (f), *house, home.*

	SINGULAR	PLURAL
Nom.	dom**us**	dom**ūs**
Voc.	dom**us**	dom**ūs**
Acc.	dom**um**	dom**ūs** (dom**ōs**)
Gen.	dom**ūs**	dom**uum** (dom**ōrum**)
Dat.	dom**uī**	dom**ibus**
Abl.	dom**ō**	dom**ibus**

16. Fifth Declension

Fifth Declension Nouns end in **–ēs** in the Nominative Singular.

diēs – diēī (m), *day.* **rēs – reī** (f), *thing.*

	SINGULAR	PLURAL	SINGULAR	PLURAL
Nom.	di**ēs**	di**ēs**	**rēs**	**rēs**
Voc.	di**ēs**	di**ēs**	**rēs**	**rēs**
Acc.	di**em**	di**ēs**	**rem**	**rēs**
Gen.	di**ēī**	di**ērum**	**reī**	**rērum**
Dat.	di**ēī**	di**ēbus**	**reī**	**rēbus**
Abl.	di**ē**	di**ēbus**	**rē**	**rēbus**

II. ADJECTIVES AND ADVERBS

Latin Adjectives can be arranged in **two** groups, those with First and Second Declension endings, and those with Third Declension endings.

17. First and Second Declension Adjectives

altus-a-um, *high, deep.*

	SINGULAR			PLURAL		
	M	*F*	*N*	*M*	*F*	*N*
Nom.	alt**us**	alt**a**	alt**um**	alt**ī**	alt**ae**	alt**a**
Voc.	alt**e**	alt**a**	alt**um**	alt**ī**	alt**ae**	alt**a**
Acc.	alt**um**	alt**am**	alt**um**	alt**ōs**	alt**ās**	alt**a**
Gen.	alt**ī**	alt**ae**	alt**ī**	alt**ōrum**	alt**ārum**	alt**ōrum**
Dat.	alt**ō**	alt**ae**	alt**ō**	alt**īs**	alt**īs**	alt**īs**
Abl.	alt**ō**	alt**ā**	alt**ō**	alt**īs**	alt**īs**	alt**īs**

miser-misera-miserum, *wretched.*

	SINGULAR			PLURAL		
	M	*F*	*N*	*M*	*F*	*N*
N.	miser	misera	miserum	miserī	miserae	misera
V.	miser	misera	miserum	miserī	miserae	misera
A.	miserum	miseram	miserum	miserōs	miserās	misera
G.	miserī	miserae	miserī	miserōrum	miserārum	miserōrum
D.	miserō	miserae	miserō	miserīs	miserīs	miserīs
A.	miserō	miserā	miserō	miserīs	miserīs	miserīs

Declined like miser, i.e. keep the **e** are,

asper – aspera – asperum, *rough*
līber – lībera – līberum, *free*
tener – tenera – tenerum, *tender.*

niger – nigra – nigrum, *black.*

	SINGULAR			PLURAL		
	M	*F*	*N*	*M*	*F*	*N*
Nom.	niger	nigra	nigrum	nigrī	nigrae	nigra
Voc.	niger	nigra	nigrum	nigrī	nigrae	nigra
Acc.	nigrum	nigram	nigrum	nigrōs	nigrās	nigra
Gen.	nigrī	nigrae	nigrī	nigrōrum	nigrārum	nigrōrum
Dat.	nigrō	nigrae	nigrō	nigrīs	nigrīs	nigrīs
Abl.	nigrō	nigrā	nigrō	nigrīs	nigrīs	nigrīs

Declined like niger, i.e. drop the **e** are,

aeger – aegra – aegrum, *sick*
pulcher – pulchra – pulchrum, *beautiful*
crēber – crēbra – crēbrum, *frequent*
piger – pigra – pigrum, *lazy.*

18. ūllus – ūlla – ūllum, *any.*

	SINGULAR			PLURAL		
	M	*F*	*N*	*M*	*F*	*N*
Nom.	ūllus	ūlla	ūllum	ūllī	ūllae	ūlla
Acc.	ūllum	ūllam	ūllum	ūllōs	ūllās	ūlla
Gen.	ūllīus	ūllīus	ūllīus	ūllōrum	ūllārum	ūllōrum
Dat.	ūllī	ūllī	ūllī	ūllīs	ūllīs	ūllīs
Abl.	ūllō	ūllā	ūllō	ūllīs	ūllīs	ūllīs

Declined like ūllus are,

nūllus	**– a**	**– um,** *no, none*
ūnus	**– a**	**– um,** *one*
sōlus	**– a**	**– um,** *alone, only*
tōtus	**– a**	**– um,** *whole of*
alius	**– a**	**– ud,** *another*
uter	**– utra**	**– utrum,** *which of two*
uterque	**– utraque**	**– utrumque,** *each of two*
neuter	**– neutra**	**– neutrum,** *neither of two*
alter	**– altera**	**– alterum,** *the one, the other of two.*

19. Third Declension Adjectives

(*a*) Adjectives with **one** ending in the **Nominative Singular.**

ingēns – ingēns – ingēns, *huge.*

	SINGULAR			PLURAL		
	M	*F*	*N*	*M*	*F*	*N*
Nom.	ingē**ns**	ingē**ns**	ingē**ns**	ingent**ēs**	ingent**ēs**	ingent**ia**
Voc.	ingē**ns**	ingē**ns**	ingē**ns**	ingent**ēs**	ingent**ēs**	ingent**ia**
Acc.	ingent**em**	ingent**em**	ingē**ns**	ingent**ēs**	ingent**ēs**	ingent**ia**
Gen.	ingent**is**	ingent**is**	ingent**is**	ingent**ium**	ingent**ium**	ingent**ium**
Dat.	ingent**ī**	ingent**ī**	ingent**ī**	ingent**ibus**	ingent**ibus**	ingent**ibus**
Abl.	ingent**ī**	ingent**ī**	ingent**ī**	ingent**ibus**	ingent**ibus**	ingent**ibus**

fēlīx – fēlīx – fēlīx, *happy.*

	SINGULAR			PLURAL		
	M	*F*	*N*	*M*	*F*	*N*
Nom.	fēlī**x**	fēlī**x**	fēlī**x**	fēlīc**ēs**	fēlīc**ēs**	fēlīc**ia**
Voc.	fēlī**x**	fēlī**x**	fēlī**x**	fēlīc**ēs**	fēlīc**ēs**	fēlīc**ia**
Acc.	fēlīc**em**	fēlīc**em**	fēlī**x**	fēlīc**ēs**	fēlīc**ēs**	fēlīc**ia**
Gen.	fēlīc**is**	fēlīc**is**	fēlīc**is**	fēlīc**ium**	fēlīc**ium**	fēlīc**ium**
Dat.	fēlīc**ī**	fēlīc**ī**	fēlīc**ī**	fēlīc**ibus**	fēlīc**ibus**	fēlīc**ibus**
Abl.	fēlīc**ī**	fēlīc**ī**	fēlīc**ī**	fēlīc**ibus**	fēlīc**ibus**	fēlīc**ibus**

Declined like ingēns or fēlīx are,

audāx, *bold*
ferōx, *fierce*
sapiēns, *wise*
prūdēns, *prudent*
trux, *grim.*

(*b*) Adjectives with **two** endings in the **Nominative Singular.**

brevis – brevis – breve, *short, brief.*

	SINGULAR			PLURAL		
	M	*F*	*N*	*M*	*F*	*N*
Nom.	brev**is**	brev**is**	brev**e**	brev**ēs**	brev**ēs**	brev**ia**
Voc.	brev**is**	brev**is**	brev**e**	brev**ēs**	brev**ēs**	brev**ia**
Acc.	brev**em**	brev**em**	brev**e**	brev**ēs**	brev**ēs**	brev**ia**
Gen.	brev**is**	brev**is**	brev**is**	brev**ium**	brev**ium**	brev**ium**
Dat.	brev**ī**	brev**ī**	brev**ī**	brev**ibus**	brev**ibus**	brev**ibus**
Abl.	brev**ī**	brev**ī**	brev**ī**	brev**ibus**	brev**ibus**	brev**ibus**

Declined like brevis are,

facilis, *easy*
difficilis, *difficult*
fortis, *brave*
levis, *light*
gravis, *heavy*
omnis, *all, every*
dulcis, *sweet*
trīstis, *sad*
tālis, *such a kind*
quālis, *what kind of.*

(*c*) Adjectives with **three** endings in the **Nominative Singular.**

celer – celeris – celere, *swift.*

	SINGULAR			PLURAL		
	M	*F*	*N*	*M*	*F*	*N*
Nom.	cel**er**	celer**is**	celer**e**	celer**ēs**	celer**ēs**	celer**ia**
Voc.	cel**er**	celer**is**	celer**e**	celer**ēs**	celer**ēs**	celer**ia**
Acc.	celer**em**	celer**em**	celer**e**	celer**ēs**	celer**ēs**	celer**ia**
Gen.	celer**is**	celer**is**	celer**is**	celer**ium**	celer**ium**	celer**ium**
Dat.	celer**ī**	celer**ī**	celer**ī**	celer**ibus**	celer**ibus**	celer**ibus**
Abl.	celer**ī**	celer**ī**	celer**ī**	celer**ibus**	celer**ibus**	celer**ibus**

ācer – ācris – ācre, *keen.*

	SINGULAR			PLURAL		
	M	*F*	*N*	*M*	*F*	*N*
Nom.	āc**er**	ācr**is**	ācr**e**	ācr**ēs**	ācr**ēs**	acr**ia**
Voc.	āc**er**	ācr**is**	ācr**e**	ācr**ēs**	ācr**ēs**	acr**ia**
Acc.	ācr**em**	ācr**em**	ācr**e**	ācr**ēs**	ācr**ēs**	acr**ia**
Gen.	ācr**is**	ācr**is**	ācr**is**	ācr**ium**	ācr**ium**	ācr**ium**
Dat.	ācr**ī**	ācr**ī**	ācr**ī**	ācr**ibus**	ācr**ibus**	ācr**ibus**
Abl.	ācr**ī**	ācr**ī**	ācr**ī**	ācr**ibus**	ācr**ibus**	ācr**ibus**

(*d*) Exceptions

vetus – vetus – vetus, *old.*

	SINGULAR			PLURAL		
	M	*F*	*N*	*M*	*F*	*N*
Nom.	vet**us**	vet**us**	vet**us**	veter**ēs**	veter**ēs**	veter**a**
Voc.	vet**us**	vet**us**	vet**us**	veter**ēs**	veter**ēs**	veter**a**
Acc.	veter**em**	veter**em**	vet**us**	veter**ēs**	veter**ēs**	veter**a**
Gen.	veter**is**	veter**is**	veter**is**	veter**um**	veter**um**	veter**um**
Dat.	veter**ī**	veter**ī**	veter**ī**	veter**ibus**	veter**ibus**	veter**ibus**
Abl.	veter**e**	veter**e**	veter**e**	veter**ibus**	veter**ibus**	veter**ibus**

Declined like vetus are,

pauper – pauperis, *poor*
dīves – dīvitis, *rich*
} no Neuter.

(*e*) The **Present Participle** declines like **ingēns.** If it is used as an Adjective, its Ablative Singular is **–ī**; if it is used as a pure participle, i.e. in an Ablative Absolute, its Ablative Singular is **–e.**

e.g. ā puerō errant**ī** – *by the wandering boy*
vēre ineunt**e** – *at the approach of spring.*

(*f*) *Declension of the Comparative*

pulchrior – pulchrior – pulchrius, *more beautiful.*

	SINGULAR		
	M	*F*	*N*
Nom.	pulchr**ior**	pulchr**ior**	pulchr**ius**
Voc.	pulchr**ior**	pulchr**ior**	pulchr**ius**
Acc.	pulchriōr**em**	pulchriōr**em**	pulchr**ius**
Gen.	pulchriōr**is**	pulchriōr**is**	pulchriōr**is**
Dat.	pulchriōr**ī**	pulchriōr**ī**	pulchriōr**ī**
Abl.	pulchriōr**e**	pulchriōr**e**	pulchriōr**e**

	PLURAL		
	M	*F*	*N*
Nom.	pulchriōr**ēs**	pulchriōr**ēs**	pulchriōr**a**
Voc.	pulchriōr**ēs**	pulchriōr**ēs**	pulchriōr**a**
Acc.	pulchriōr**ēs**	pulchriōr**ēs**	pulchriōr**a**
Gen.	pulchriōr**um**	pulchriōr**um**	pulchriōr**um**
Dat.	pulchriōr**ibus**	pulchriōr**ibus**	pulchriōr**ibus**
Abl.	pulchriōr**ibus**	pulchriōr**ibus**	pulchriōr**ibus**

(*g*) The following rule may be observed.

Third Declension Adjectives have their Ablative Singular in **–ī**

Nominative, Vocative and Accusative Neuter Plural in **–ia**

Genitive Plural in **–ium.**

Except, dīves, pauper, vetus and all Comparatives which have their

Ablative Singular in **–e**

Nominative, Vocative and Accusative Neuter Plural in **–a**

Genitive Plural in **–um.**

20. Comparison of Adjectives

To form the **Comparative** of the regular Adjective change the –ī or –**is** of the Masculine Genitive Singular into **–ior** and into –**issimus** to form the **Superlative.**

(*a*)

POSITIVE	COMPARATIVE	SUPERLATIVE	
altus	alt**ior**	alt**issimus**	*high*
prūdēns	prūdent**ior**	prūdent**issimus**	*prudent*
ferōx	ferōc**ior**	ferōc**issimus**	*fierce*
dulcis	dulc**ior**	dulc**issimus**	*sweet*

(*b*) If the Adjective ends in **–er** in the Masculine Nominative Singular, double the **–r** and add –**imus** to form the **Superlative.**

POSITIVE	COMPARATIVE	SUPERLATIVE	
miser	miser**ior**	miser**rimus**	*wretched*
pulcher	pulchr**ior**	pulcher**rimus**	*beautiful*
ācer	ācr**ior**	ācer**rimus**	*keen*
celer	celer**ior**	celer**rimus**	*swift*

(*c*) There are **six** Adjectives ending in **–ilis** which double the **–l** and change the **–is** into –**imus** to form the **Superlative.**

	POSITIVE	COMPARITIVE	SUPERLATIVE	
	facilis	facil**ior**	facil**limus**	*easy*
	difficilis	difficil**ior**	difficil**limus**	*difficult*
	similis	simil**ior**	simil**limus**	*similar*
	dissimilis	dissimil**ior**	dissimil**limus**	*dissimilar*
	gracilis	gracil**ior**	gracil**limus**	*slender*
	humilis	humil**ior**	humil**limus**	*humble*
But	nōbilis	nōbil**ior**	nōbil**issimus**	*noble*
	ūtilis	ūtil**ior**	ūtil**issimus**	*useful*

(*d*) *Irregular Comparison*

POSITIVE	COMPARATIVE	SUPERLATIVE	
bonus	**melior**	**optimus**	*good*
malus	**pēior**	**pessimus**	*bad*
multus	**plūs**	**plūrimus**	*much*
multī	**plūrēs**	**plūrimī**	*many*
magnus	**māior**	**maximus**	*great*
parvus	**minor**	**minimus**	*small*
dubius	**magis dubius**	**maximē dubius**	*doubtful*
idōneus	**magis idōneus**	**maximē idōneus**	*suitable*

N.B. If the Adjective ends in **-us** preceded by a vowel, it compares with **magis** and **maximē**, but **antīquus,** *ancient* is regular.

antīquus	antīqu**ior**	antīqu**issimus**	*ancient*

21. Comparison of Adverbs

The **Comparative** of an **Adverb** is the **same** as the **Neuter Nominative Singular** of the **Comparative Adjective.** To form the **Superlative,** change the –**us** of the **Superlative Adjective** into –**ē.**

(*a*)

POSITIVE	COMPARATIVE	SUPERLATIVE	
ferōciter	ferō**cius**	ferōcissimē	*fiercely*
facile	facil**ius**	facillimē	*easily*
difficulter	difficil**ius**	difficillimē	*with difficulty*
miserē	miser**ius**	miserrimē	*wretchedly*
ācriter	ācr**ius**	ācerrimē	*keenly*

(*b*)

POSITIVE	COMPARATIVE	SUPERLATIVE	
bene	mel**ius**	optimē	*well*
male	pē**ius**	pessimē	*badly*
magnopere	**magis**	maximē	*greatly*
paulum	min**us**	minimē	*little*
saepe	saep**ius**	saepissimē	*often*
diū	diū**tius**	diūtissimē	*for a long time*
prope	prop**ius**	proximē	*near*

III. PRONOUNS

22. (*a*) **ego**, *I.* **tū**, *you.*

	SINGULAR	PLURAL	SINGULAR	PLURAL
Nom.	**ego**	**nōs**	**tū**	**vōs**
Acc.	**mē**	**nōs**	**tē**	**vōs**
Gen.	**meī**	**nostrum, nostrī**	**tuī**	**vestrum, vestrī**
Dat.	**mihi**	**nōbīs**	**tibi**	**vōbīs**
Abl.	**mē**	**nōbīs**	**tē**	**vōbīs**

meus – a – um, *my* **noster – tra – trum,** *our*

tuus – a – um, *your* **vester – tra – trum,** *your*

(*b*) **is – ea – id,** *he, she, it, that.*

	SINGULAR			PLURAL		
	M	*F*	*N*	*M*	*F*	*N*
Nom.	**is**	**ea**	**id**	**eī**	**eae**	**ea**
Acc.	**eum**	**eam**	**id**	**eōs**	**eās**	**ea**
Gen.	**ēius**	**ēius**	**ēius**	**eōrum**	**eārum**	**eōrum**
Dat.	**eī**	**eī**	**eī**	**eīs**	**eīs**	**eīs**
Abl.	**eō**	**eā**	**eō**	**eīs**	**eīs**	**eīs**

N.B. ēius means *his, her, its;* **eōrum,** etc., means *their;* **suus – a – um** means *his own,* etc.

(*c*) **hīc – haec – hōc,** *this.*

	SINGULAR			PLURAL		
	M	*F*	*N*	*M*	*F*	*N*
Nom.	**hīc**	**haec**	**hōc**	**hī**	**hae**	**haec**
Acc.	**hunc**	**hanc**	**hōc**	**hōs**	**hās**	**haec**
Gen.	**hūius**	**hūius**	**hūius**	**hōrum**	**hārum**	**hōrum**
Dat.	**huīc**	**huīc**	**huīc**	**hīs**	**hīs**	**hīs**
Abl.	**hōc**	**hāc**	**hōc**	**hīs**	**hīs**	**hīs**

(*d*) **ille – illa – illud,** *that.*

	SINGULAR			PLURAL		
	M	*F*	*N*	*M*	*F*	*N*
Nom.	**ille**	**illa**	**illud**	**illī**	**illae**	**illa**
Acc.	**illum**	**illam**	**illud**	**illōs**	**illās**	**illa**
Gen.	**illīus**	**illīus**	**illīus**	**illōrum**	**illārum**	**illōrum**
Dat.	**illī**	**illī**	**illī**	**illīs**	**illīs**	**illīs**
Abl.	**illō**	**illā**	**illō**	**illīs**	**illīs**	**illīs**

(*e*) **īdem – eadem – idem,** *the same.*

	SINGULAR			PLURAL		
	M	*F*	*N*	*M*	*F*	*N*
Nom.	**ī**dem	**ea**dem	**i**dem	**eī**dem	**eae**dem	**ea**dem
Acc.	**eun**dem	**ean**dem	**i**dem	**eōs**dem	**eās**dem	**ea**dem
Gen.	**ēius**dem	**ēius**dem	**ēius**dem	**eōrun**dem	**eārun**dem	**eōrun**dem
Dat.	**eī**dem	**eī**dem	**eī**dem	**eīs**dem	**eīs**dem	**eīs**dem
Abl.	**eō**dem	**eā**dem	**eō**dem	**eīs**dem	**eīs**dem	**eīs**dem

(*f*) **mē,** *myself.* **tē,** *yourself.* **nōs,** *ourselves.* **vōs,** *yourselves.*

Acc.	**mē**	**tē**	**nōs**	**vōs**
Gen.	**meī**	**tuī**	**nostrī, nostrum**	**vestrum, vestrī**
Dat.	**mihi**	**tibi**	**nōbīs**	**vōbīs**
Abl.	**mē**	**tē**	**nōbīs**	**vōbīs**

sē, *himself, herself, themselves.*

Acc.	**sē**
Gen.	**suī**
Dat.	**sibi**
Abl.	**sē**

(*g*) **ipse – ipsa – ipsum,** *self.*

	SINGULAR			PLURAL		
	M	*F*	*N*	*M*	*F*	*N*
Nom.	ips**e**	ips**a**	ips**um**	ips**ī**	ips**ae**	ips**a**
Acc.	ips**um**	ips**am**	ips**um**	ips**ōs**	ips**ās**	ips**a**
Gen.	ips**īus**	ips**īus**	ips**īus**	ips**ōrum**	ips**ārum**	ips**ōrum**
Dat.	ips**ī**	ips**ī**	ips**ī**	ips**īs**	ips**īs**	ips**īs**
Abl.	ips**ō**	ips**ā**	ips**ō**	ips**īs**	ips**īs**	ips**īs**

(*h*) **quī – quae – quod,** *who, which.*

	SINGULAR			PLURAL		
	M	*F*	*N*	*M*	*F*	*N*
Nom.	quī	quae	quod	quī	quae	quae
Acc.	quem	quam	quod	quōs	quās	quae
Gen.	cūius	cūius	cūius	quōrum	quārum	quōrum
Dat.	cuī	cuī	cuī	quibus	quibus	quibus
Abl.	quō	quā	quō	quibus	quibus	quibus

N.B. quīdam – quaedam – quoddam, *a certain*
quīcunque – quaecunque – quodcunque, *whoever.*
The Interrogative Adjective
quī / **quis** } – **quae – quod,** *what, which?*
decline like **quī – quae – quod**

(*i*) **quis – quis – quid,** *who, what?*

	SINGULAR			PLURAL		
	M	*F*	*N*	*M*	*F*	*N*
Nom.	quis	quis	quid	quī	quae	quae
Acc.	quem	quam	quid	quōs	quās	quae
Gen.	cūius	cūius	cūius	quōrum	quārum	quōrum
Dat.	cuī	cuī	cuī	quibus	quibus	quibus
Abl.	quō	quā	quō	quibus	quibus	quibus

N.B. aliquis – aliqua – aliquid, *someone*
quisquis – quisquis – quid / **c** } **quid,** *whoever*
quisquam – quisquam – quicquam, *anyone*
quisque – quisque – quid / **c** } **que,** *each*
are declined like **quis – quis – quid**

(*j*) **nēmō,** *no one.*

Nom.	nēmō
Acc.	nēminem
Gen.	**nūllīus**
Dat.	nēminī
Abl.	**nūllō**

IV. VERBS

23. Latin Verbs are divided into four groups called **Conjugations.** Every regular Verb has four principal parts from which all other parts may be formed.

First Conjugation: **amō – amāre – amāvī – amātum,** *to love.*

Second Conjugation: **moneō – monēre – monuī – monitum,** *to warn.*

Third Conjugation: **regō – regere – rēxī – rēctum,** *to rule.*

Fourth Conjugation: **audiō – audīre – audīvī – audītum,** *to hear.*

There is also another group of Verbs ending in **–io** which belong to the Third Conjugation:
e.g. **capiō – capere – cēpī – captum,** *to capture.*

Every regular Verb has three stems.

(1) The **Present Stem** is obtained by cutting off the **–re** from the **Present Infinitive Active.**
e.g. **amā~~re~~ monē~~re~~ rege~~re~~ audī~~re~~**

(2) The **Perfect Stem** is obtained by cutting off the **–ī** from the **Perfect Indicative Active.**
e.g. **amāv~~ī~~ monu~~ī~~ rēx~~ī~~ audīv~~ī~~**

(3) The **Supine Stem** is obtained by cutting off the **–um** from the **Supine** (Fourth Part).
e.g. **amāt~~um~~ monit~~um~~ rēct~~um~~ audīt~~um~~**

The **Present Stem** is used to form the following parts:

Present, Future, Imperfect } Indicative Active and Passive

Present, Imperfect } Subjunctive Active and Passive

Present Imperative Active and Passive

Present Infinitive Active and Passive

Present Participle, Gerund and Gerundive.

The **Perfect Stem** is used to form the following parts:

Perfect and Pluperfect Indicative and Subjunctive Active
Future Perfect Indicative Active
Perfect Infinitive Active

The **Supine Stem** is used to form the following parts:

Perfect and Pluperfect Indicative and Subjunctive Passive
Future Perfect Indicative Passive
Perfect Infinitive and Participle Passive
Future Infinitive Active and Passive and Future Participle

24. (*a*) *First Conjugation Indicative Active and Passive*

amō – amāre – amāvī – amātum, *to love.*

PRESENT		PERFECT	
ACTIVE	PASSIVE	ACTIVE	PASSIVE
am**ō**	am**or**	amāv**ī**	amāt**us sum**
am**ās**	am**āris**	amāv**istī**	amāt**us es**
am**at**	am**ātur**	amāv**it**	amāt**us est**
am**āmus**	am**āmur**	amāv**imus**	amāt**ī sumus**
am**ātis**	am**āminī**	amāv**istis**	amāt**ī estis**
am**ant**	am**antur**	amāv**ērunt**	amāt**ī sunt**
FUTURE		FUTURE PERFECT	
amāb**ō**	amāb**or**	amāv**erō**	amāt**us erō**
amāb**is**	amāb**eris**	amāv**eris**	amāt**us eris**
amāb**it**	amāb**itur**	amāv**erit**	amāt**us erit**
amāb**imus**	amāb**imur**	amāv**erimus**	amāt**ī erimus**
amāb**itis**	amāb**iminī**	amāv**eritis**	amāt**ī eritis**
amāb**unt**	amāb**untur**	amāv**erint**	amāt**ī erunt**
IMPERFECT		PLUPERFECT	
amā**bam**	amā**bar**	amāv**eram**	amāt**us eram**
amā**bas**	amā**bāris**	amāv**erās**	amāt**us erās**
amā**bat**	amā**bātur**	amāv**erat**	amāt**us erat**
amā**bāmus**	amā**bāmur**	amāv**erāmus**	amāt**ī erāmus**
amā**bātis**	amā**bāminī**	amāv**erātis**	amāt**ī erātis**
amā**bant**	amā**bantur**	amāv**erant**	amāt**ī erant**

(*b*) *Second Conjugation Indicative Active and Passive*

monēo – monēre – monuī – monitum, *to warn.*

PRESENT		PERFECT	
ACTIVE	PASSIVE	ACTIVE	PASSIVE
mone**ō**	mone**or**	monu**ī**	monit**us sum**
mon**ēs**	mon**ēris**	monu**istī**	monit**us es**
mon**et**	mon**ētur**	monu**it**	monit**us est**
mon**ēmus**	mon**ēmur**	monu**imus**	monitī **sumus**
mon**ētis**	mon**ēminī**	monu**istis**	monitī **estis**
mon**ent**	mon**entur**	monu**ērunt**	monitī **sunt**

FUTURE		FUTURE PERFECT	
monē**bō**	monē**bor**	monu**erō**	monit**us erō**
monē**bis**	monē**beris**	monu**eris**	monit**us eris**
monē**bit**	monē**bitur**	monu**erit**	monit**us erit**
monē**bimus**	monē**bimur**	monu**erimus**	monitī **erimus**
monē**bitis**	monē**biminī**	monu**eritis**	monitī **eritis**
monē**bunt**	monē**buntur**	monu**erint**	monitī **erunt**

IMPERFECT		PLUPERFECT	
monē**bam**	monē**bar**	monu**eram**	monit**us eram**
monē**bās**	monē**bāris**	monu**erās**	monit**us erās**
monē**bat**	monē**bātur**	monu**erat**	monit**us erat**
monē**bāmus**	monē**bāmur**	monu**erāmus**	monitī **erāmus**
monē**bātis**	monē**bāminī**	monu**erātis**	monitī **erātis**
monē**bant**	monē**bantur**	monu**erant**	monitī **erant**

(*c*) *Third Conjugation Indicative Active and Passive*

regō – regĕre – rēxī – rēctum, *to rule.*

PRESENT		PERFECT	
ACTIVE	PASSIVE	ACTIVE	PASSIVE
reg**ō**	reg**or**	rēx**ī**	rēct**us sum**
reg**is**	reg**eris**	rēx**istī**	rēct**us es**
reg**it**	reg**itur**	rēx**it**	rēct**us est**
reg**imus**	reg**imur**	rēx**imus**	rēctī **sumus**
reg**itis**	reg**iminī**	rēx**istis**	rēctī **estis**
reg**unt**	reg**untur**	rēx**ērunt**	rēctī **sunt**

FUTURE		FUTURE PERFECT	
regam	regar	rēxerō	rēctus erō
regēs	regēris	rēxeris	rēctus eris
reget	regētur	rēxerit	rēctus erit
regēmus	regēmur	rēxerimus	rēctī erimus
regētis	regēminī	rēxeritis	rēctī eritis
regent	regentur	rēxerint	rēctī erunt

IMPERFECT		PLUPERFECT	
regēbam	regēbar	rēxeram	rēctus eram
regēbās	regēbāris	rēxerās	rēctus erās
regēbat	regēbātur	rēxerat	rēctus erat
regēbāmus	regēbāmur	rēxerāmus	rēctī erāmus
regēbātis	regēbāminī	rēxerātis	rēctī erātis
regēbant	regēbantur	rēxerant	rēctī erant

(*d*) *Fourth Conjugation Indicative Active and Passive*

audiō – audīre – audīvī – audītum, *to hear.*

PRESENT		PERFECT	
ACTIVE	PASSIVE	ACTIVE	PASSIVE
audiō	audior	audīvī	audītus sum
audīs	audīris	audīvistī	audītus es
audit	audītur	audīvit	audītus est
audīmus	audīmur	audīvimus	audītī sumus
audītis	audīminī	audīvistis	audītī estis
audiunt	audiuntur	audīvērunt	audītī sunt

FUTURE		FUTURE PERFECT	
audiam	audiar	audīverō	audītus erō
audiēs	audiēris	audīveris	audītus eris
audiet	audiētur	audīverit	audītus erit
audiēmus	audiēmur	audīverimus	audītī erimus
audiētis	audiēminī	audīveritis	audītī eritis
audient	audientur	audīverint	audītī erunt

IMPERFECT		PLUPERFECT	
audiēbam	audiēbar	audīveram	audītus eram
audiēbās	audiēbāris	audīverās	audītus erās
audiēbat	audiēbātur	audīverat	audītus erat
audiēbāmus	audiēbāmur	audīverāmus	audītī erāmus
audiēbātis	audiēbāminī	audīverātis	audītī erātis
audiēbant	audiēbantur	audīverant	audītī erant

(*e*) *Third Conjugation* **-io** *Indicative Active and Passive*

capiō – capere – cēpī – captum, *to capture.*

PRESENT		PERFECT	
ACTIVE	PASSIVE	ACTIVE	PASSIVE
capiō	capior	cēpī	captus sum
capis	caperis	cēpistī	captus es
capit	capitur	cēpit	captus est
capimus	capimur	cēpimus	captī sumus
capitis	capiminī	cēpistis	captī estis
capiunt	capiuntur	cēpērunt	captī sunt
FUTURE		FUTURE PERFECT	
capiam	capiar	cēperō	captus erō
capiēs	capiēris	cēperis	captus eris
capiet	capiētur	cēperit	captus erit
capiēmus	capiēmur	cēperimus	captī erimus
capiētis	capiēminī	cēperitis	captī eritis
capient	capientur	cēperint	captī erunt
IMPERFECT		PLUPERFECT	
capiēbam	capiēbar	cēperam	captus eram
capiēbās	capiēbāris	cēperās	captus erās
capiēbat	capiēbātur	cēperat	captus erat
capiēbāmus	capiēbāmur	cēperāmus	captī erāmus
capiēbātis	capiēbāminī	cēperātis	captī erātis
capiēbant	capiēbantur	cēperant	captī erant

25. (*a*) *First Conjugation Subjunctive Active and Passive*

PRESENT		PERFECT	
ACTIVE	PASSIVE	ACTIVE	PASSIVE
amem	amer	amāverim	amātus sim
amēs	amēris	amāveris	amātus sīs
amet	amētur	amāverit	amātus sit
amēmus	amēmur	amāverimus	amātī sīmus
amētis	amēminī	amāveritis	amātī sītis
ament	amentur	amāverint	amātī sint

IMPERFECT		PLUPERFECT	
am**ārem**	am**ārer**	amāv**issem**	amāt**us essem**
am**ārēs**	am**ārēris**	amāv**issēs**	amāt**us essēs**
am**āret**	am**ārētur**	amāv**isset**	amāt**us esset**
am**ārēmus**	am**ārēmur**	amāv**issēmus**	amātī **essēmus**
am**ārētis**	am**ārēminī**	amāv**issētis**	amātī **essētis**
am**ārent**	am**ārentur**	amāv**issent**	amātī **essent**

(b) Second Conjugation Subjunctive Active and Passive

PRESENT		PERFECT	
ACTIVE	PASSIVE	ACTIVE	PASSIVE
mon**eam**	mon**ear**	monu**erim**	monit**us sim**
mon**eās**	mon**eāris**	monu**eris**	monit**us sīs**
mon**eat**	mon**eātur**	monu**erit**	monit**us sit**
mon**eāmus**	mon**eāmur**	monu**erimus**	monitī **sīmus**
mon**eātis**	mon**eāminī**	monu**eritis**	monitī **sītis**
mon**eant**	mon**eantur**	monu**erint**	monitī **sint**

IMPERFECT		PLUPERFECT	
mon**ērem**	mon**ērer**	monu**issem**	monit**us essem**
mon**ērēs**	mon**ērēris**	monu**issēs**	monit**us essēs**
mon**ēret**	mon**ērētur**	monu**isset**	monit**us esset**
mon**ērēmus**	mon**ērēmur**	monu**issēmus**	monitī **essēmus**
mon**ērētis**	mon**ērēminī**	monu**issētis**	monitī **essētis**
mon**ērent**	mon**ērentur**	monu**issent**	monitī **essent**

(c) Third Conjugation Subjunctive Active and Passive

PRESENT		PERFECT	
ACTIVE	PASSIVE	ACTIVE	PASSIVE
reg**am**	reg**ar**	rēx**erim**	rēct**us sim**
reg**ās**	reg**āris**	rēx**eris**	rēct**us sīs**
reg**at**	reg**ātur**	rēx**erit**	rēct**us sit**
reg**āmus**	reg**āmur**	rēx**erimus**	rēctī **sīmus**
reg**ātis**	reg**āminī**	rēx**eritis**	rēctī **sītis**
reg**ant**	reg**antur**	rēx**erint**	rēctī **sint**

IMPERFECT		PLUPERFECT	
regerem	regerer	rēxissem	rēctus essem
regerēs	regerēris	rēxissēs	rēctus essēs
regeret	regerētur	rēxisset	rēctus esset
regerēmus	regerēmur	rēxissēmus	rēctī essēmus
regerētis	regerēminī	rēxissētis	rēctī essētis
regerent	regerentur	rēxissent	rēctī essent

(*d*) *Fourth Conjugation Subjunctive Active and Passive*

PRESENT		PERFECT	
ACTIVE	PASSIVE	ACTIVE	PASSIVE
audiam	audiar	audīverim	audītus sim
audiās	audiāris	audīveris	audītus sīs
audiat	audiātur	audīverit	audītus sit
audiāmus	audiāmur	audīverimus	audītī sīmus
audiātis	audiāminī	audīveritis	audītī sītis
audiant	audiantur	audīverint	audītī sint

IMPERFECT		PLUPERFECT	
audīrem	audīrer	audīvissem	audītus essem
audīrēs	audīrēris	audīvissēs	audītus essēs
audīret	audīrētur	audīvisset	audītus esset
audīrēmus	audīrēmur	audīvissēmus	audītī essēmus
audīrētis	audīrēminī	audīvissētis	audītī essētis
audīrent	audīrentur	audīvissent	audītī essent

(*e*) *Third Conjugation* **-io** *Subjunctive Active and Passive*

PRESENT		PERFECT	
ACTIVE	PASSIVE	ACTIVE	PASSIVE
capiam	capiar	cēperim	captus sim
capiās	capiāris	cēperis	captus sīs
capiat	capiātur	cēperit	captus sit
capiāmus	capiāmur	cēperimus	captī sīmus
capiātis	capiāminī	cēperitis	captī sītis
capiant	capiantur	cēperint	captī sint

IMPERFECT		PLUPERFECT	
cap**erem**	cap**erer**	cēp**issem**	capt**us essem**
cap**erēs**	cap**erēris**	cēp**issēs**	capt**us essēs**
cap**eret**	cap**erētur**	cēp**isset**	capt**us esset**
cap**erēmus**	cap**erēmur**	cēp**issēmus**	capt**ī essēmus**
cap**erētis**	cap**erēminī**	cēp**issētis**	capt**ī essētis**
cap**erent**	cap**erentur**	cēp**issent**	capt**ī essent**

26. *Imperative Active and Passive All Conjugations*

ACTIVE

FIRST	SECOND	THIRD	FOURTH	-IO
am**ā**	mon**ē**	reg**e**	aud**ī**	cap**e**
am**āte**	mon**ēte**	reg**ite**	aud**īte**	cap**ite**

PASSIVE

FIRST	SECOND	THIRD	FOURTH	-IO
am**āre**	mon**ēre**	reg**ere**	aud**īre**	cap**ere**
am**āminī**	mon**ēminī**	reg**iminī**	aud**īminī**	cap**iminī**

27. *Infinitive Active and Passive All Conjugations*

ACTIVE

	FIRST	SECOND	THIRD	FOURTH
Present	am**āre**	mon**ēre**	reg**ere**	aud**īre**
Future	amāt**ūrus esse**	monit**ūrus esse**	rēct**ūrus esse**	audīt**ūrus esse**
Perfect	amāv**isse**	monu**isse**	rēx**isse**	audīv**isse**

-IO

Present	cap**ere**
Future	capt**ūrus esse**
Perfect	cēp**isse**

PASSIVE

	FIRST	SECOND	THIRD	FOURTH	-IO
Present	am**ārī**	mon**ērī**	reg**ī**	aud**īrī**	cap**ī**
Future	amāt**um īrī**	monit**um īrī**	rēct**um īrī**	audīt**um īrī**	capt**um īrī**
Perfect	amāt**us esse**	monit**us esse**	rēct**us esse**	audīt**us esse**	capt**us esse**

28. *Participles Active and Passive All Conjugations*

ACTIVE

	FIRST	SECOND	THIRD
Present	am**āns–āns–āns**	mon**ēns–ēns–ēns**	reg**ēns–ēns–ēns**
Future	amāt**ūrus–a–um**	monit**ūrus–a–um**	rēct**ūrus–a–um**

	FOURTH	-IO
Present	aud**iēns–iēns–iēns**	cap**iēns–iēns–iēns**
Future	audīt**ūrus–a–um**	capt**ūrus–a–um**

PASSIVE

	FIRST	SECOND	THIRD	FOURTH
Perfect	amāt**us–a–um**	monit**us–a–um**	rēct**us–a–um**	audīt**us–a–um**

	-IO
Perfect	capt**us–a–um**

29. *Gerund and Gerundive All Conjugations*

	FIRST	SECOND	THIRD
Gerund	am**andum**	mon**endum**	reg**endum**
Gerundive	am**andus–a–um**	mon**endus–a–um**	reg**endus–a–um**

	FOURTH	-IO
Gerund	aud**iendum**	cap**iendum**
Gerundive	aud**iendus–a–um**	cap**iendus–a–um**

30. Latin also has the following irregular Verbs which do not conform to any conjugation.

sum – esse – fuī, *to be*
possum – posse – potuī, *to be able*
volō – velle – voluī, *to wish, to be willing*
nōlō – nōlle – nōluī, *to be unwilling*
mālō – mālle – māluī, *to prefer*
eō – īre – īvī – itum, *to go*

ferō – ferre – tulī – lātum, *to bear, carry*
fīō – fierī – factus sum, *to be made, to become.*

31. **sum – esse – fuī,** *to be.*

INDICATIVE		SUBJUNCTIVE	
PRESENT	PERFECT	PRESENT	PERFECT
sum	fuī	sim	fuerim
es	fuistī	sīs	fueris
est	fuit	sit	fuerit
sumus	fuimus	sīmus	fuerimus
estis	fuistis	sītis	fueritis
sunt	fuērunt	sint	fuerint

FUTURE	FUTURE PERFECT
erō	fuerō
eris	fueris
erit	fuerit
erimus	fuerimus
eritis	fueritis
erunt	fuerint

IMPERFECT	PLUPERFECT	IMPERFECT	PLUPERFECT
eram	fueram	essem	fuissem
erās	fuerās	essēs	fuissēs
erat	fuerat	esset	fuisset
erāmus	fuerāmus	essēmus	fuissēmus
erātis	fuerātis	essētis	fuissētis
erant	fuerant	essent	fuissent

IMPERATIVE	INFINITIVES	PARTICIPLE
es	Present **esse**	Future **futūrus-a-um**
este	Future **futūrus esse (fore)**	
	Perfect **fuisse**	

N.B. The following compound Verbs conjugate like sum.

absum – abesse – āfuī, *to be distant*
adsum – adesse – adfuī, *to be present*
dēsum – dēesse – dēfuī, *to fail, be lacking to* + Dative
īnsum – inesse – īnfui, *to be in*
intersum – interesse – interfuī, *to take part in* + Dative
praesum – praeesse – praefuī, *to be in command of* + Dative
obsum – obesse – obfuī, *to be of disadvantage to* + Dative
supersum – superesse – superfuī, *to survive* + Dative

But prōsum – prōdesse – prōfuī, *to be of advantage to* + Dative puts in a **–d** where any part of **sum** begins with an **–e.**

e.g. prōsum	Future: prō**d**erō
prōdes	etc.
prōdest	

32. **possum – posse – potuī,** *to be able, can.*

N.B. This verb is really a compound of **pot** + sum. Where any part of **sum** begins with an –**s**, pot becomes po**s**.

INDICATIVE		SUBJUNCTIVE	
PRESENT	PERFECT	PRESENT	PERFECT
pos**sum**	potuī	poss**im**	potu**erim**
pot**es**	potu**istī**	poss**īs**	potu**eris**
pot**est**	potu**it**	poss**it**	potu**erit**
pos**sumus**	potu**imus**	poss**īmus**	potu**erimus**
pot**estis**	potu**istis**	poss**ītis**	potu**eritis**
pos**sunt**	potu**ērunt**	poss**int**	potu**erint**

FUTURE	FUTURE PERFECT
pot**erō**	potu**erō**
pot**eris**	potu**eris**
pot**erit**	potu**erit**
pot**erimus**	potu**erimus**
pot**eritis**	potu**eritis**
pot**erunt**	potu**erint**

IMPERFECT	PLUPERFECT	IMPERFECT	PLUPERFECT
pot**eram**	potu**eram**	poss**em**	potu**issem**
pot**erās**	potu**erās**	poss**ēs**	potu**issēs**
pot**erat**	potu**erat**	poss**et**	potu**isset**
pot**erāmus**	potu**erāmus**	poss**ēmus**	potu**issēmus**
pot**erātis**	potu**erātis**	poss**ētis**	potu**issētis**
pot**erant**	potu**erant**	poss**ent**	potu**issent**

INFINITIVES

Present	**posse**
Perfect	potu**isse**

33. **volō – velle – voluī,** *to be willing, to wish.*

INDICATIVE / SUBJUNCTIVE

PRESENT	PERFECT	PRESENT	PERFECT
vol**ō**	volu**ī**	vel**im**	volu**erim**
vī**s**	volu**istī**	vel**īs**	volu**eris**
vu**lt**	volu**it**	vel**it**	volu**erit**
vol**umus**	volu**imus**	vel**īmus**	volu**erimus**
vul**tis**	volu**istis**	vel**ītis**	volu**eritis**
vol**unt**	volu**ērunt**	vel**int**	volu**erint**

FUTURE	FUTURE PERFECT
vol**am**	volu**erō**
vol**ēs**	volu**eris**
vol**et**	volu**erit**
vol**ēmus**	volu**erimus**
vol**ētis**	volu**eritis**
vol**ent**	volu**erint**

IMPERFECT	PLUPERFECT	IMPERFECT	PLUPERFECT
volē**bam**	volu**eram**	vell**em**	volu**issem**
volē**bās**	volu**erās**	vell**ēs**	volu**issēs**
volē**bat**	volu**erat**	vell**et**	volu**isset**
volē**bāmus**	volu**erāmus**	vell**ēmus**	volu**issēmus**
volē**bātis**	volu**erātis**	vell**ētis**	volu**issētis**
volē**bant**	volu**erant**	vell**ent**	volu**issent**

INFINITIVES		PARTICIPLE	
Present	**velle**	Present	vol**ens–ēns–ēns**
Perfect	volu**isse**		

34. **nōlō – nōlle – nōluī**, *to be unwilling.*

INDICATIVE		SUBJUNCTIVE	
PRESENT	PERFECT	PRESENT	PERFECT
nōl**ō**	nōlu**ī**	nōl**im**	nōlu**erim**
nōn v**īs**	nōlu**istī**	nōl**īs**	nōlu**eris**
nōn vul**t**	nōlu**it**	nōl**it**	nōlu**erit**
nōl**umus**	nōlu**imus**	nōl**īmus**	nōlu**erimus**
nōn vul**tis**	nōlu**istis**	nōl**ītis**	nōlu**eritis**
nōl**unt**	nōlu**ērunt**	nōl**int**	nōlu**erint**

FUTURE	FUTURE PERFECT
nōl**am**	nōlu**erō**
nōl**ēs**	nōlu**eris**
nōl**et**	nōlu**erit**
nōl**ēmus**	nōlu**erimus**
nōl**ētis**	nōlu**eritis**
nōl**ent**	nōlu**erint**

IMPERFECT	PLUPERFECT	IMPERFECT	PLUPERFECT
nōlē**bam**	nōlu**eram**	nōll**em**	nōlu**issem**
nōlē**bās**	nōlu**erās**	nōll**ēs**	nōlu**issēs**
nōlē**bat**	nōlu**erat**	nōll**et**	nōlu**isset**
nōlē**bāmus**	nōlu**erāmus**	nōll**ēmus**	nōlu**issēmus**
nōlē**bātis**	nōlu**erātis**	nōll**ētis**	nōlu**issētis**
nōlē**bant**	nōlu**erant**	nōll**ent**	nōlu**issent**

IMPERATIVE	INFINITIVES		PARTICIPLE	
nōl**ī**	Present	**nōlle**	Present	nōl**ēns–ēns–ēns**
nōl**īte**	Perfect	nōlu**isse**		

35. **mālo – mālle – māluī**, *to prefer.*

INDICATIVE		SUBJUNCTIVE	
PRESENT	PERFECT	PRESENT	PERFECT
māl**ō**	mālu**ī**	māl**im**	mālu**erim**
māv**īs**	mālu**istī**	māl**īs**	mālu**eris**
māvul**t**	mālu**it**	māl**it**	mālu**erit**
māl**umus**	mālu**imus**	māl**īmus**	mālu**erimus**
māvul**tis**	mālu**istis**	māl**ītis**	mālu**eritis**
māl**unt**	mālu**ērunt**	māl**int**	mālu**erint**

FUTURE	FUTURE PERFECT
māl**am**	māl**uerō**
māl**ēs**	māl**ueris**
māl**et**	māl**uerit**
māl**ēmus**	māl**uerimus**
māl**ētis**	māl**ueritis**
māl**ent**	māl**uerint**

IMPERFECT	PLUPERFECT	IMPERFECT	PLUPERFECT
mālē**bam**	māl**ueram**	māll**em**	māl**uissem**
mālē**bās**	māl**uerās**	māll**ēs**	māl**uissēs**
mālē**bat**	māl**uerat**	māll**et**	māl**uisset**
mālē**bāmus**	māl**uerāmus**	māll**ēmus**	māl**uissēmus**
mālē**bātis**	māl**uerātis**	māll**ētis**	māl**uissētis**
mālē**bant**	māl**uerant**	māll**ent**	māl**uissent**

INFINITIVES

Present	**mālle**
Perfect	māl**uisse**

36. eō – īre – īvī – itum, *to go.*

INDICATIVE		SUBJUNCTIVE	
PRESENT	PERFECT	PRESENT	PERFECT
eō	**īvī**	**eam**	**īverim**
is	**īvistī**	**eās**	**īveris**
it	**īvit**	**eat**	**īverit**
īmus	**īvimus**	**eāmus**	**īverimus**
ītis	**īvistis**	**eātis**	**īveritis**
eunt	**īvērunt**	**eant**	**īverint**

FUTURE	FUTURE PERFECT
ībō	**īverō**
ībis	**īveris**
ībit	**īverit**
ībimus	**īverimus**
ībitis	**īveritis**
ībunt	**īverint**

IMPERFECT	PLUPERFECT	IMPERFECT	PLUPERFECT
ībam	**īveram**	**īrem**	**īvissem**
ībās	**īverās**	**īrēs**	**īvissēs**
ībat	**īverat**	**īret**	**īvisset**
ībāmus	**īverāmus**	**īrēmus**	**īvissēmus**
ībātis	**īverātis**	**īrētis**	**īvissētis**
ībant	**īverant**	**īrent**	**īvissent**

IMPERATIVE	INFINITIVES		PARTICIPLES	
ī	Present	**īre**	Present	**iēns-iēns-iēns (euntis)**
īte	Future	**itūrus esse**	Future	**itūrus-a-um**
	Perfect	**īvisse**		
	Gerund		**eundum**	
	Gerundive		**eundum** (impersonal)	

N.B. The following compound Verbs are conjugated like **eō,** but drop the **v** in their third part.

abeō – abīre – abiī – abitum, *to go away*
adeō – adīre – adiī – aditum, *to approach*
exeō – exīre – exiī – exitum, *to go out*
ineō – inīre – iniī – initum, *to enter*
intereō – interīre – interiī – interitum, *to perish*
obeō – obīre – obiī – obitum, *meet, die*
pereō – perīre – periī – peritum, *to perish*
redeō – redīre – rediī – reditum, *to return*
trānseō – trānsīre – trānsiī – trānsitum, *to cross.*

37. **ferō – ferre – tulī – lātum,** *to bear, carry.*

INDICATIVE

PRESENT		PERFECT	
ACTIVE	PASSIVE	ACTIVE	PASSIVE
fer**ō**	fer**or**	tul**ī**	lāt**us sum**
fer**s**	fer**ris**	tul**istī**	lāt**us es**
fer**t**	fer**tur**	tul**it**	lāt**us est**
fer**imus**	fer**imur**	tul**imus**	lāt**ī sumus**
fer**tis**	fer**iminī**	tul**istis**	lāt**ī estis**
fer**unt**	fer**untur**	tul**ērunt**	lāt**ī sunt**

FUTURE		FUTURE PERFECT	
fer**am**	fer**ar**	tul**erō**	lā**tus erō**
fer**ēs**	fer**ēris**	tul**eris**	lā**tus eris**
fer**et**	fer**ētur**	tul**erit**	lā**tus erit**
fer**ēmus**	fer**ēmur**	tul**erimus**	lātī **erimus**
fer**ētis**	fer**ēminī**	tul**eritis**	lātī **eritis**
fer**ent**	fer**entur**	tul**erint**	lātī **erunt**

IMPERFECT		PLUPERFECT	
ACTIVE	PASSIVE	ACTIVE	PASSIVE
ferē**bam**	ferē**bar**	tul**eram**	lā**tus eram**
ferē**bās**	ferē**bāris**	tul**erās**	lā**tus erās**
ferē**bat**	ferē**bātur**	tul**erat**	lā**tus erat**
ferē**bāmus**	ferē**bāmur**	tul**erāmus**	lātī **erāmus**
ferē**bātis**	ferē**bāminī**	tul**erātis**	lātī **erātis**
ferē**bant**	ferē**bantur**	tul**erant**	lātī **erant**

SUBJUNCTIVE

PRESENT		PERFECT	
fer**am**	fer**ar**	tul**erim**	lā**tus sim**
fer**ās**	fer**āris**	tul**eris**	lā**tus sīs**
fer**at**	fer**ātur**	tul**erit**	lā**tus sit**
fer**āmus**	fer**āmur**	tul**erimus**	lātī **sīmus**
fer**ātis**	fer**āminī**	tul**eritis**	lātī **sītis**
fer**ant**	fer**antur**	tul**erint**	lātī **sint**

IMPERFECT		PLUPERFECT	
ferr**em**	ferr**er**	tul**issem**	lā**tus essem**
ferr**ēs**	ferr**ēris**	tul**issēs**	lā**tus essēs**
ferr**et**	ferr**ētur**	tul**isset**	lā**tus esset**
ferr**ēmus**	ferr**ēmur**	tul**issēmus**	lātī **essēmus**
ferr**ētis**	ferr**ēminī**	tul**issētis**	lātī **essētis**
ferr**ent**	ferr**entur**	tul**issent**	lātī **essent**

IMPERATIVE			INFINITIVES	
ACTIVE	PASSIVE		ACTIVE	PASSIVE
fe**r**	fer**re**	Present	fer**re**	fer**rī**
fer**te**	fer**iminī**	Future	lā**tūrus esse**	lā**tum īrī**
		Perfect	**tulisse**	lā**tus esse**

PARTICIPLES

Present	ferēns-ēns-ēns	Gerund	ferendum
Future	lātūrus-a-um	Gerundive	ferendus-a-um
Perfect	lātus-a-um		

N.B. The following compound Verbs conjugate like fero.

afferō – afferre – attulī – allātum, *to bring to*
auferō – auferre – abstulī – ablātum, *to take away*
cōnferō – cōnferre – contulī – collātum, *to bring together*
efferō – efferre – extulī – ēlātum, *to bring out*
referō – referre – rettulī – relātum, *to bring back.*

38. **fīō – fierī – factus sum,** *to be made, to become.*

INDICATIVE PRESENT	INDICATIVE PERFECT	SUBJUNCTIVE PRESENT	SUBJUNCTIVE PERFECT
fīō	factus sum	fīam	factus sim
fīs	factus es	fīās	factus sīs
fit	factus est	fīat	factus sit
—	factī sumus	fīāmus	factī sīmus
—	factī estis	fīātis	factī sītis
fīunt	factī sunt	fīant	factī sint

FUTURE	FUTURE PERFECT
fīam	factus erō
fīēs	factus eris
fīet	factus erit
fīēmus	factī erimus
fīētis	factī eritis
fīent	factī erunt

IMPERFECT	PLUPERFECT	IMPERFECT	PLUPERFECT
fīēbam	factus eram	fierem	factus essem
fīēbās	factus erās	fierēs	factus essēs
fīēbat	factus erat	fieret	factus esset
fīēbāmus	factī erāmus	fierēmus	factī essēmus
fīēbātis	factī erātis	fierētis	factī essētis
fīēbant	factī erant	fierent	factī essent

INFINITIVES / PARTICIPLE

Present	fierī	Perfect	factus-a-um
Future	factum īrī		
Perfect	factus esse	Gerundive	faciendus-a-um

39. *Deponent Verbs*

These Verbs are **Active** in meaning, but **Passive** in form except for the **Present Participle**, **Future Infinitive**, **Future Participle** } which are **Active** in form.

N.B. The **Perfect Participle** of a **Deponent Verb** is **Active** in meaning.

(*a*) *First Conjugation*

hortor – hortārī – hortātus sum, *to encourage.*

INDICATIVE		SUBJUNCTIVE	
PRESENT	PERFECT	PRESENT	PERFECT
hort**or**	hortāt**us sum**	hort**er**	hortāt**us sim**
hort**āris**	hortāt**us es**	hort**ēris**	hortāt**us sīs**
etc.	etc.	etc.	etc.

FUTURE	FUTURE PERFECT
hortā**bor**	hortāt**us erō**
hortā**beris**	hortāt**us eris**
etc.	etc.

IMPERFECT	PLUPERFECT	IMPERFECT	PLUPERFECT
hortā**bar**	hortāt**us eram**	hortār**er**	hortāt**us essem**
hortā**bāris**	hortāt**us erās**	hortār**ēris**	hortāt**us essēs**
etc.	etc.	etc.	etc.

IMPERATIVE	INFINITIVES	
hort**āre**	Present	hort**ārī**
hort**āminī**	Future	hortāt**ūrus esse**
	Perfect	hortāt**us esse**

PARTICIPLES

Present	hort**āns-āns-āns**	Gerund	hort**andum**
Future	hortāt**ūrus-a-um**	Gerundive	hort**andus–a–um**
Perfect	hortāt**us-a-um** (**Active** in meaning)		

(*b*) *Second Conjugation*

vereor – verērī – veritus sum, *to fear.*

INDICATIVE		SUBJUNCTIVE	
PRESENT	PERFECT	PRESENT	PERFECT
vere**or**	verit**us sum**	vere**ar**	verit**us sim**
ver**ēris**	verit**us es**	vere**āris**	verit**us sīs**
etc.	etc.	etc.	etc.

FUTURE	FUTURE PERFECT
verē**bor**	verit**us erō**
verē**beris**	verit**us eris**
etc.	etc.

IMPERFECT	PLUPERFECT	IMPERFECT	PLUPERFECT
verē**bar**	verit**us eram**	verē**rer**	verit**us essem**
verē**bāris**	verit**us erās**	verē**rēris**	verit**us essēs**
etc.	etc.	etc.	etc.

IMPERATIVE	INFINITIVES	
ver**ēre**	Present	ver**ērī**
ver**ēminī**	Future	verit**ūrus esse**
	Perfect	verit**us esse**

PARTICIPLES			
Present	ver**ēns-ēns-ēns**	Gerund	ver**endum**
Future	verit**ūrus-a-um**	Gerundive	ver**endus-a-um**
Perfect	verit**us-a-um** (**Active** in meaning)		

(*c*) *Third Conjugation*

proficīscor – proficīscī – profectus sum, *to set out.*

INDICATIVE		SUBJUNCTIVE	
PRESENT	PERFECT	PRESENT	PERFECT
proficīsc**or**	profect**us sum**	proficīsc**ar**	profect**us sim**
proficīsc**eris**	profect**us es**	proficīsc**āris**	profect**us sīs**
etc.	etc.	etc.	etc.

FUTURE	FUTURE PERFECT
proficīsc**ar**	profect**us erō**
proficīsc**ēris**	profect**us eris**
etc.	etc.

IMPERFECT	PLUPERFECT	IMPERFECT	PLUPERFECT
proficīscē**bar**	profect**us eram**	proficīscer**er**	profect**us essem**
proficīscē**bāris**	profect**us erās**	proficīscer**ēris**	profect**us essēs**
etc.	etc.	etc.	etc.

IMPERATIVE	INFINITIVES	
proficīsc**ere**	Present	proficīsc**ī**
proficīsc**iminī**	Future	profect**ūrus esse**
	Perfect	profect**us esse**

PARTICIPLES			
Present	proficīsc**ēns-ēns-ēns**	Gerund	proficīsc**endum**
Future	profect**ūrus-a-um**	Gerundive	proficīsc**endum**
Perfect	profect**us-a-um**		(Impersonal)
	(**Active** in meaning)		

(*d*) *Fourth Conjugation*

mentior – mentīrī – mentītus sum, *to tell a lie.*

INDICATIVE		SUBJUNCTIVE	
PRESENT	PERFECT	PRESENT	PERFECT
ment**ior**	mentīt**us sum**	ment**iar**	mentīt**us sim**
ment**īris**	mentīt**us es**	ment**iāris**	mentīt**us sīs**
etc.	etc.	etc.	etc.

FUTURE	FUTURE PERFECT
ment**iar**	mentīt**us erō**
ment**iēris**	mentīt**us eris**
etc.	etc.

IMPERFECT	PLUPERFECT	IMPERFECT	PLUPERFECT
ment**iēbar**	mentīt**us eram**	mentīr**er**	mentīt**us essem**
ment**iēbāris**	mentīt**us erās**	mentīr**ēris**	mentīt**us essēs**
etc.	etc.	etc.	etc.

IMPERATIVE	INFINITIVES	
ment**īre**	Present	ment**īrī**
ment**īminī**	Future	mentīt**ūrus esse**
	Perfect	mentīt**us esse**

PARTICIPLES			
Present	ment**iēns-iēns-iēns**	Gerund	ment**iendum**
Future	mentīt**ūrus-a-um**	Gerundive	ment**iendum**
Perfect	mentīt**us-a-um**		(Impersonal)
	(**Active** in meaning)		

(*e*) *Third Conjugation* – **ior**

morior – morī – mortuus sum, *to die.*

INDICATIVE		SUBJUNCTIVE	
PRESENT	PERFECT	PRESENT	PERFECT
mor**ior**	mort**uus sum**	mor**iar**	mort**uus sim**
mor**eris**	mort**uus es**	mor**iāris**	mort**uus sīs**
etc.	etc.	etc.	etc.

FUTURE	FUTURE PERFECT
mor**iar**	mort**uus erō**
mor**iēris**	mort**uus eris**
etc.	etc.

IMPERFECT	PLUPERFECT	IMPERFECT	PLUPERFECT
mor**iēbar**	mort**uus eram**	more**rer**	mort**uus essem**
mor**iēbāris**	mort**uus eras**	more**rēris**	mort**uus essēs**
etc.	etc.	etc.	etc.

IMPERATIVE	INFINITIVES	
mor**ere**	Present	mor**ī**
mor**iminī**	Future	mor**itūrus esse**
	Perfect	mort**uus esse**

PARTICIPLES

Present	mor**iēns-iēns-iēns**	Gerund	mor**iendum**
Future	mor**itūrus-a-um**	Gerundive	mor**iendum**
Perfect	mort**uus-a-um**		(Impersonal)
	(**Active** in meaning)		

40. *Semi-Deponent Verbs*

Latin has four Verbs **Active** in meaning which are **Active** in form in the **Present, Future and Imperfect tenses,** but **Passive** in form in the **Perfect Tenses.**

audeō – audēre – ausus sum, *to dare*
gaudeō – gaudēre – gāvīsus sum, *to rejoice*
soleō – solēre – solitus sum, *to be accustomed to*
(cōn)fīdō – fīdĕre – fīsus sum, *to trust.*

e.g.

INDICATIVE		SUBJUNCTIVE	
PRESENT	PERFECT	PRESENT	PERFECT
aude**ō**	ausus **sum**	aude**am**	ausus **sim**
aud**ēs**	ausus **ēs**	aude**ās**	ausus **sīs**
etc.	etc.	etc.	etc.

FUTURE	FUTURE PERFECT
audē**bō**	ausus **erō**
audē**bis**	ausus **eris**
etc.	etc.

IMPERFECT	PLUPERFECT	IMPERFECT	PLUPERFECT
audē**bam**	ausus **eram**	audē**rem**	ausus **essem**
audē**bās**	ausus **erās**	audē**rēs**	ausus **essēs**
etc.	etc.	etc.	etc.

IMPERATIVE	INFINITIVES	
aud**ē**	Present	aud**ēre**
aud**ēte**	Future	aus**ūrus esse**
	Perfect	aus**us esse**

PARTICIPLES

Present	aud**ēns-ēns-ēns**	Gerund	aud**endum**
Future	aus**ūrus-a-um**	Gerundive	aud**endus-a-um**
Perfect	aus**us-a-um** (**Active** in meaning)		

V. PREPOSITIONS

41. *With Accusative*

ad: to, towards, at, with regard to, about (of numbers)

ad castra redīre: *to return to the camp.*

ad iānuam manēre: *to stay at the door.*

ad virtūtem: *with regard to courage.*

ad tempus: *in time.*

ad centum: *about an hundred.*

ante: before

ante portam: *before the gate.*

ante prīmam lūcem: *before dawn.*

apud: at the house of, in the writings of, before (of persons)

apud mē: *at my house.*

apud Cicerōnem: *in the writings of Cicero.*

apud iūdicem: *before the judge.*

contrā: against, opposite to

contrā hostēs: *against the enemy.*

īnsula contrā Britanniam sita: *an island* {*opposite Britain.* / *lying off Britain.*}

extrā: outside of

extrā tēlī iactum: *out of range.*

extrā ordinem: *out of turn.*

extrā urbem: *outside the city.*

in: into, against

in Italiam: *into Italy.*

in hostēs impetum facere: *to make an attack* {*against* / *on* / *upon*} *the enemy.*

inter: between, among, during

inter rīpās: *between the banks.*

inter sē pugnābant: *they fought with each other.*

inter proelium: *during the battle.*

intrā: within

intrā moenia: *within the walls.*

intrā tēlī iactum: *within range.*

ob: on account of

quam ob rem: *therefore.*

ob hanc causam: *for this reason.*

per: through, during, by means of, by (in oaths)

per mediam urbem: *through the middle of the city.*

per noctem: *during the night.*

per servum: *by means of a slave.*

per ego tē deōs ōrō: *I beg you by the gods.*

post: behind, after

post tergum: *in the rear.*

post hominum memoriam: *within human memory.*

praeter: past, beyond, except, contrary to

praeter urbem: *past the city.*

praeter spem: *beyond expectation.*
praeter ducem: *except the general.*
praeter cōnsuētūdinem: *contrary to custom.*

prope: near
prope casam: *near the cottage.*

propter: on account of
propter vulnera: *on account of the wounds.*

secundum: in accordance with
{secundum flūmen / secundō flūmine}: *downstream.*

sub: under (of motion), **immediately after**
sub iugum mittere: *to send under the yoke.*
sub bellum: *immediately after the war.*

trāns: across
trāns flūmen: *across the river.*

ultrā: beyond
ultrā collem: *beyond the hill.*

42. *With Ablative*

a(b): by, from, in relation to
ā mīlite: *by the soldier.*
ā Rōmā decem mīlia passuum abest: *he is ten miles distant from Rome.*
ā puerō: *from boyhood.*
ā tergō, fronte, latere: *in the rear, front, flank.*
ā Caesare stāre: *to be on the side of Caesar.*

cum: with, along with
mēcum festīnā: *hurry with me.*
cum librīs ad ludum veniet: *he will come to school with his books.*
summā cum vī: *with the utmost force.*

dē: down from, about, according to
dē ponte: *down from the bridge.*
dē pāce agere: *to discuss peace.*
dē industriā: *on purpose.*
dē mōre: *according to custom.*
dē imprōvīsō: *unexpectedly.*
dē integrō: *afresh.*

ē(x): from, out of, according to

ē Britanniā nāvigāre: *to sail from Britain.*
ē castrīs exīre: *to go out of the camp.*
ē senātūs cōnsultō: *according to the decree of the senate.*
sex ē mīlitibus: *six of the soldiers.*
statua ex aurō facta: *a statue made of gold.*

in: in, on, in the case of

in urbe manēre: *to stay in the city.*
in capite vulnerārī: *to be wounded on the head.*
in Cicerōne: *in the case of Cicero.*

pro: on behalf of, in front of, in proportion to, as

prō patriā: *on behalf of one's country.*
prō castrīs: *in front of the camp.*
prō virīlī parte pugnāre: *to fight to the best of one's ability.*
prō inimīcō tē habeō: *I regard you as an enemy.*

sine: without

sine scūtō: *without a shield.*

sub: under

sub marī: *under the sea.*
sub hastā vendere: *to sell at an auction.*
sub corōnā vendere: *to sell as a slave.*

VI. NUMBERS

43.

		CARDINAL	ORDINAL
1	I	ūn**us-a-um**	prīm**us-a-um**
2	II	du**o-ae-o**	secund**us-a-um** (alter)
3	III	**trēs-ēs-ia**	terti**us-a-um**
4	IV	quattuor	quart**us-a-um**
5	V	quīnque	quīnt**us-a-um**
6	VI	sex	sext**us-a-um**
7	VII	septem	septim**us-a-um**
8	VIII	octō	octāv**us-a-um**
9	IX	novem	nōn**us-a-um**
10	X	decem	decim**us-a-um**
11	XI	ūndecim	ūndecim**us-a-um**

		CARDINAL	ORDINAL
12	XII	duodecim	duodecim**us-a-um**
13	XIII	tredecim	terti**us** decim**us-a-um**
14	XIV	quattuordecim	quart**us** decim**us-a-um**
15	XV	quīndecim	quīnt**us** decim**us-a-um**
16	XVI	sēdecim	sext**us** decim**us-a-um**
17	XVII	septendecim	septim**us** decim**us-a-um**
18	XVIII	duodēvīgintī	duodēvīcēsim**us-a-um**
19	XIX	ūndēvīgintī	ūndēvīcēsim**us-a-um**
20	XX	vīgintī	vīcēsim**us-a-um**
21	XXI	vīgintī ūn**us** (ūn**us** et vīgintī)	vīcēsim**us** prīm**us** (ūn**us** et vīcēsim**us**)
22	XXII	vīgintī du**o** (du**o** et vīgintī)	vīcēsim**us** secund**us** (alt**er** et vicēsim**us**)
30	XXX	trī**gintā**	trīcēsim**us**
40	XL	quadrā**gintā**	quadrāgēsim**us**
50	L	quīnquā**gintā**	quīnquāgēsim**us**
60	LX	sexā**gintā**	sexāgēsim**us**
70	LXX	septuā**gintā**	septuāgēsim**us**
80	LXXX	octō**gintā**	octōgēsim**us**
90	XC	nōnā**gintā**	nōnāgēsim**us**
100	C	centum	centēsim**us**
200	CC	ducent**ī-ae-a**	ducentēsim**us**
300	CCC	trecent**ī-ae-a**	trecentēsim**us**
400	CCCC	quadrin**gentī-ae-a**	quadringentēsim**us**
500	D(IƆ)	quīn**gentī-ae-a**	quīngentēsim**us**
600	DC	sesc**entī-ae-a**	sescentēsim**us**
700	DCC	septin**gentī-ae-a**	septingentēsim**us**
800	DCCC	octin**gentī-ae-a**	octingentēsim**us**
900	DCCCC	nōn**gentī-ae-a**	nōngentēsim**us**
1000	M(CIƆ)	mīlle	mīllēsim**us**
2000	MM	du**o** mīl**ia**	bis mīllēsim**us**

N.B. (i) The numbers, **1, 2, 3** are declinable, **4 to 100** are indeclinable. For the declension of **ūnus** vid. sec. 18.

	duo – duae – duo			trēs – trēs – tria		
	M	*F*	*N*	*M*	*F*	*N*
Nom.	duo	du**ae**	duo	tr**ēs**	tr**ēs**	tr**ia**
Acc.	du**ōs** (duo)	du**ās**	duo	tr**ēs**	tr**ēs**	tr**ia**
Gen.	du**ōrum**	du**ārum**	du**ōrum**	tr**ium**	tr**ium**	tr**ium**
Dat.	du**ōbus**	du**ābus**	du**ōbus**	tr**ibus**	tr**ibus**	tr**ibus**
Abl.	du**ōbus**	du**ābus**	du**ōbus**	tr**ibus**	tr**ibus**	tr**ibus**

ambo – ambae – ambo, *both* declines like **duo**

(ii) Mīlle, *a thousand* is indeclinable, but **mīlia,** *thousands* declines thus:

Nom.	mīl**ia**
Acc.	mīl**ia**
Gen.	mīl**ium**
Dat.	mīl**ibus**
Abl.	mīl**ibus**

Mīlia is always followed by the Genitive.
e.g. cum mīlle nōngentīs nōnāgintā novem mīlitibus; *with 1,999 soldiers.*
but, cum duōbus mīlibus **mīlitum**; *with 2,000 soldiers.*

VII. DATES

44. (*a*) *Names of the Months*

Iānuār**ius-a-um**	(Ian.)	Iūl**ius-a-um**	(Iul.)
Februār**ius-a-um**	(Feb.)	August**us-a-um**	(Aug.)
Mart**ius-a-um**	(Mart.)	Septemb**er-bris-bre**	(Sept.)
Aprīl**is-is-e**	(Apr.)	Octōb**er-bris-bre**	(Oct.)
Māi**us-a-um**	(Mai.)	Novemb**er-bris-bre**	(Nov.)
Iūn**ius-a-um**	(Iun.)	Decemb**er-bris-bre**	(Dec.)

July and August were also known as Quīntīl**is-is-e** and Sextīl**is-is-e.**

(b) Divisions of the Months

Kalend**ae-ārum** (f. pl.)	1st of every month.
Nōn**ae-ārum** (f. pl.)	5th of the month, except in March, July, October, May when the Nones fell on the 7th day.
Īdūs-uum (f. pl.)	13th of the month, except in March, July, October, May when the Ides fell on the 15th day.

(c) How to express a date in Latin

(i) If the date to be expressed falls on one of the divisions use a plain **Ablative** of **Time.**

e.g. *1st Dec.* Kal. Dec. (Kalendīs Decembribus)
15th March. Id. Mart. (Īdibus Martiīs)

(ii) If the date to be expressed falls on the day before one of the divisions use **prīd.** (**prīdiē**) thus:

4th Feb. **prīd.** Nōn. Feb. (**prīdiē** Nōnās Februāriās)

(iii) If the date to be expressed falls between one of the divisions, subtract the English date from the date of the **next** Latin division, and since the Romans counted inclusively **add one** (**add** on **two** when calculating to the **Kalends** of the **next** month).

e.g. *9th Dec.* **a.d.V.** Īd. Dec.
(ante diem quīntum Īdūs Decembrēs)
16th April. **a.d.XVI** Kal. Māi.
(ante diem sextum decimum Kalendās Māiās)

N.B. Never write a.d.II. This means you have missed a division.

Additional Accidence

VIII. NOUNS

45. *Second Declension*

(*a*) Nouns ending in **-ius** or **-ium** have their **Genitive Singular** in **-ī** or **-iī.**

e.g. **fīlius,** has fīlī or fīliī
praemium, has praemī or praemiī

(*b*) Many cities and countries ending in **-us** are **Feminine.**

e.g. Corinth**us,** *Corinth*
Aegypt**us,** *Egypt*

Humus, *the ground* is also **Feminine,** but **pelagus,** *sea* and **vulgus,** *mob* are **Neuter.**

(*c*) **Sēstertius,** *sesterce* (a coin) has a contracted **Genitive Plural,** sēsterti**um.** This form of the Genitive Plural is very common in poetry, e.g. de**um** for deōrum, vir**um** for virōrum. It is also found in the Genitive Plural of the hundreds, e.g. ducent**um.**

(*d*) **Locus-ī** (m), *place* has two Plurals, loc**a**-ōrum (n), *places, localities,* and loc**ī**-ōrum (m), *topics, passages in a book.*

46. *Third Declension*

(*a*) Names of towns and rivers ending in **-is** have their **Accusative Singular** in **-im** and their **Ablative Singular** in **-ī.**

e.g. **Neāpolis,** *Naples* has Neāpol**im** and Neāpol**ī**
Tiberis, *Tiber* has Tiber**im** and Tiber**ī**
Also **puppis-is** (f), *stern of a ship*
turris-is (f), *tower*
secūris-is (f), *axe*

Other nouns such as **nāvis-is** (f), *ship* and **ignis-is** (m), *fire* have both forms of the **Ablative Singular, -e** or **-ī.**

(*b*) Nouns such as **pēs-pedis** (m), *foot*, **pāx-pācis** (f), *peace*, **ōs-ōris** (n), *mouth* do **not** belong to the Monosyllabic Group as their stems do not end in two consonants and therefore have **-um** in the **Genitive Plural.**

(*c*) **Mānēs** (m pl), *spirits of the dead*, and **Penātēs** (m pl) *household gods*, have their Genitive Plural in **-ium.**

(*d*) Note the following nouns:

mel-**mellis** (n), *honey*
iter-**itineris** (n), *journey*
carō-**carnis** (f), *flesh*
trabs-**trabis** (f), *beam*
lac-**lactis** (n), *milk*
pecus-**pecudis** (f), *beast*
supellex-**supellectilis** (f), *furniture*
rūs-**rūris** (n), *country*
nix-**nivis** (f), *snow*
aes-**aeris** (n), *bronze*
genus-**generis** (n), *race, kind*
tellūs-**tellūris** (f), *land*
seges-**segetis** (f), *crop*
cor-**cordis** (n), *heart*
pecus-**pecoris** (n), *herd*
fur-**furis** (m), *thief*
plēbs-**plēbis** (f), *common people*
palūs-**palūdis** (f), *marsh*

(*e*) In poetry the **Accusative Plural** of Third Declension Nouns and Adjectives with Genitive Plural in **-ium** is often written as **-īs,** e.g. omn**īs**, font**īs**.

47. *Fourth Declension*
The following Nouns have their **Dative** and **Ablative Plural** in **-ubus**:

acus–ūs (f), *needle*
arcus–ūs (m), *bow*
quercus–ūs (f), *oak*
tribus–ūs (f), *tribe*

But, lacus-ūs (m), *lake* and **portus-ūs** (m) *harbour* have both **-ibus** and **-ubus.**

48. *Fifth Declension*

(*a*) Only **diēs** and **rēs** have a complete Plural.

(*b*) **Aciēs-aciēī** (f), *line of battle* and **spēs-speī** (f), *hope* have Nominative and Accusative Plural.

(*c*) The following Nouns have no Plural.

merīdiēs–diēī (m),	*midday*
fidēs–eī (f),	*faith*
plēbēs–eī (f),	*common people*

(*d*) **Diēs** is **Feminine** when it means *length of time* or *appointed day*, e.g. diē cōnstitūtā, *on a fixed day*.

(*e*) **Rēspūblica – reīpūblicae** (f), *state*, declines thus:

	SINGULAR	PLURAL
Nom.	rēspūblic**a**	rēspūblic**ae**
Acc.	re**m**pūblic**am**	rēspūblic**ās**
Gen.	re**ī**pūblic**ae**	r**ērum**pūblic**ārum**
Dat.	re**ī**pūblic**ae**	r**ēbus**pūblic**īs**
Abl.	r**ē**pūblic**ā**	r**ēbus**pūblic**īs**

49. The following nouns are found only in the **Plural:**

angustiae – ārum (f),	*narrow pass*
arma – ōrum (n),	*arms*
dīvitiae – ārum (f),	*wealth*
excubiae – ārum (f),	*watch*
fēriae – ārum (f),	*holidays*
hīberna – ōrum (n),	*winter quarters*
Kalendae – ārum (f),	*Kalends*
Idūs – uum (f),	*Ides*
īnsidiae – ārum (f),	*ambush*
līberī – ōrum (m),	*children*
minae – ārum (f),	*threats*
maiōrēs – um (m),	*ancestors*
moenia – ium (n),	*city walls*
Nōnae – ārum (f),	*Nones*
spolia – ōrum (n),	*spoils*
tenebrae – ārum (f),	*darkness*

50. The following nouns change their meaning in the **Plural:**

NOUN	SINGULAR	PLURAL
aedēs – is (f)	*temple*	*house*
auxilium – iī (n)	*help*	*auxiliary forces*
castrum – ī (n)	*fort*	*camp*
cōpia – ae (f)	*supply*	*forces*
fīnis – is (m)	*end*	*territory*
fortūna – ae (f)	*chance, fortune*	*wealth*
grātia – ae (f)	*favour*	*thanks*
impedīmentum – ī (n)	*hindrance*	*heavy baggage*
littera – ae (f)	*letter of alphabet*	*letter, dispatch, literature*
mōs – mōris (m)	*custom*	*character*
opem (f)	*help*	*resources*
pars – partis (f)	*part*	*political party*
rōstrum – ī (n)	*beak, prow*	*speaker's platform*
vīs (f)	*violence*	*strength*

51. The following nouns are indeclinable:

fās, *right, divine law*
nefās, *sin*
{**nihil** / **nil**}, *nothing*

52. In poetry Greek proper names such as **Aeneas** or **Anchises** are declined as follows:

Nom.	Aenē**ās**	Anchīs**ēs**
Voc.	Aenē**ā**	Anchīs**ē** (**ā**)
Acc.	Aenē**ān** (**am**)	Anchīs**ēn** (**am**)
Gen.	Aenē**ae**	Anchīs**ae**
Dat.	Aenē**ae**	Anchīs**ae**
Abl.	Aenē**ā**	Anchīs**ā**

IX. ADJECTIVES AND ADVERBS

53. **Uter,** *which of two,* agrees with a **Noun,** but takes the **Genitive** of a **Personal Pronoun.**

e.g. Ut**er** servus? *Which of the two slaves?*
but Uter vestr**um**? *Which of you?*

54. In poetry **Third Declension Adjectives** and **Present Participles** often have their **Genitive Plural** in **-um.**

e.g. ingent**um**, audient**um**

55.

particeps – participis, *sharing in* **superstes – superstitis,** *surviving* **sospes – sospitis,** *safe*	have their **Ablative Singular** in **-e** and their **Genitive Plural** in **-um**
inops – inopis, *in need* **memor – memoris,** *mindful*	have their **Genitive Plural** in **-um**

56. *Comparison of Adjectives*

(*a*) In addition to the Adjectives listed in sec. 20 (*d*) the following are also irregular in Comparison:

POSITIVE	COMPARATIVE	SUPERLATIVE	
benevolus	benevol**entior**	benevol**entissimus**	*kind*
magnificus	magnific**entior**	magnific**entissimus**	*noble*
dīves	dīv**itior** dī**tior**	dīv**itissimus** dī**tissimus**	*rich*
pius	**magis** pius	**maximē** pius	*pious*
vetus	vetu**stior**	vete**rrimus**	*old*
iuvenis	**iūnior** **minor nātū**	**minimus nātū**	*young*
senex	**senior** **māior nātū**	**maximus nātū**	*old*

(*b*) The following Adjectives either have no Positive or it is rarely found.

COMPARATIVE	SUPERLATIVE
exteri**or**, *outer*	extr**ēmus**, *outmost, furthest*
inter**ior**, *inner*	int**imus**, *inmost*
īnfer**ior**, *lower*	īnf**imus**, *lowest* **īmus**, *bottom of*
super**ior**, *higher*	supr**ēmus**, *final* **summus**, *top of*
poster**ior**, *later*	postr**ēmus**, *last*
pr**ior**, *former*	pr**īmus**, *first*
prop**ior**, *nearer*	prox**imus**, *nearest*
ulter**ior**, *further*	ult**imus**, *furthest, last*

(*c*) **Plūrēs,** *more* and **complūrēs,** *several* have their **Genitive Plural** in **-ium.**

57. *Further Comparison of Adverbs*

POSITIVE	COMPARATIVE	SUPERLATIVE	
citō	cit**ius**	cit**issimē**	*quickly*
nūper	—	nūper**rimē**	*recently*
—	pr**ius**, *before* / *sooner*	prīm**um**	*firstly*
		prīm**ō**	*at first*

58. The following groups contain some common Adverbs.

-am ADVERBS

cl**am**, *secretly*
pal**am**, *openly*
cōr**am**, *in the presence of*

-e ADVERBS

fer**ē**, *almost*
repent**e**, *suddenly*
vald**ē**, *exceedingly*
fort**e**, *by chance*
spont**e**, *willingly*
temer**e**, *at random, rashly*

-em ADVERBS

salt**em**, *at least*
it**em**, *likewise*

-im ADVERBS

gradāt**im**, *step by step*
paulāt**im**, *little by little*
pedetempt**im**, *gradually*
inter**im**, *meanwhile*
praesert**im**, *especially*
fūrt**im**, *stealthily*
pass**im**, *here and there*

-o ADVERBS

merit**ō**, *deservedly*
crēbr**ō**, *frequently*
subit**ō**, *suddenly*
ser**ō**, *late, too late*
tūt**ō**, *in safety*
ultr**ō**, *voluntarily*
cōnsult**ō**, *on purpose*
fals**ō**, *falsely*
continu**ō**, *forthwith*
praest**ō**, *at hand*

59. The **Accusative Singular Neuter** of many Adjectives is used as an **Adverb.**

mult**um**, *much*	nimi**um**, *too much*
paul**um**, *a little*	cēter**um**, *for the rest*
aliquant**um**, *somewhat*	prīm**um**, *firstly*
par**um**, *too little*	postrēm**um**, *finally*

60. *Table of Adverbs of Place*

	REST	TO	FROM
here	**hīc**	**hūc**	**hinc**
there	**ibī**	**eō**	**inde**
where	**ubī**	**quō**	**unde**

N.B. All Adverbs meaning *here* begin with the letter **h**.

X. PRONOUNS

61. (*a*) The suffix **-met** may be added for emphasis to all parts of **ego** except **nostrum,** to all parts of **tū** except **tū** and **vestrum,** to **sē** and **sibi,** e.g. mē**met,** tibi**met,** sē**met.**

(*b*) The form **sēsē** is found for **sē.**

(*c*) **iī** is found for eī, **iīs** for eīs, and **īsdem** for eīsdem.

62. (*a*) **Iste – ista – istud,** *that of yours,* declines like **ille.**

(*b*) The following Pronouns decline like **quī – quae – quod.**

quīvīs – quaevīs – quodvīs
quīlibet – quaelibet – quodlibet } *any you like, any one at all*
quīnam – quaenam – quodnam, *which, please?*
aliquī – aliqua – aliquod, *some*

(*c*) The following Pronouns decline like **quis – quis – quid.**

quispiam – quaepiam – quidpiam, *someone*
quisnam – quisnam – quidnam, *who please?*

(*d*) **Quis, quī** after **nē, num, sī, nisi** mean *anyone*, *any* and usually have **qua** as (i) the Nominative Feminine Singular and (ii) the Nominative and Accusative Neuter Plural.

e.g. sī **quis,** *if anyone*; sī **qua** legiō, *if any legion.*

(*e*) **Quī** is an old form of the **Ablative Singular** of **quī.** **Quīs** is an old form of the **Dative** and **Ablative Plural** of **quī.**

(*f*) **Quisque,** *each,* is written immediately after a **Numeral Adjective,** a **Superlative Adjective** and **suus.**

e.g. Fortissimus **quisque,** *all the bravest men*
Decimō **quōque** annō, *every tenth year*
Librum suum **quisque** legēbat, *each one was reading his own book*

XI. VERBS

63. As well as the Present Imperative the Latin Verb has a **Future Imperative** which is sometimes used for emphasis. It is remarkable in that it has a **Third Person.**

ACTIVE

(*a*)	FIRST	SECOND	THIRD	FOURTH
Singular	am**ātō**	mon**ētō**	reg**itō**	aud**ītō**
	am**ātō**	mon**ētō**	reg**itō**	aud**ītō**
Plural	am**ātōte**	mon**ētōte**	reg**itōte**	aud**ītōte**
	am**antō**	mon**entō**	reg**untō**	audi**untō**

PASSIVE

Singular	am**ātor**	mon**ētor**	reg**itor**	aud**ītor**
	am**ātor**	mon**ētor**	reg**itor**	aud**ītor**
	—	—	—	—
Plural	am**antor**	mon**entor**	reg**untor**	audi**untor**

(*b*) The Future Imperative of **sum.**

Singular	**estō**	Plural	**estōte**
	estō		**suntō**

(*c*) The following Verbs have a contracted **Singular** Imperative.

dīcō has **dīc**
dūcō has **dūc**
faciō has **fac**
ferō has **fer**

N.B. Their Plurals are regular, dīc**ite,** dūc**ite,** fac**ite,** fer**te.**

64. *Declension of the Gerund*

Nom.	(am**āre**)
Acc.	(am**āre**), ad am**andum**
Gen.	am**andī**
Dat.	am**andō**
Abl.	am**andō**

65. The Latin Verb has a **Second Supine** ending in **-u**, used in such phrases as,

facile dict**ū**, difficile fact**ū**, *easy to say, difficult to do*
mīrābile vīs**ū**, *amazing to see*

66. The Latin Verb has certain **Contracted Endings.**

(*a*) Second Person Singular Future and Imperfect Indicative Passive

e.g. amāb**ere** for amāberis
capiē**re** for capiēris
regēbā**re** for regēbāris

(*b*) Second Person Singular Present and Imperfect Subjunctive Passive

e.g. moneā**re** for moneāris
audīrē**re** for audīrēris

(*c*) Second Person Singular and Plural Perfect Indicative Active

e.g. amā**stī** for amāvistī
dēlē**stis** for dēlēvistis

(*d*) Third Person Plural Perfect Indicative Active

e.g. amāv**ēre** for amāvērunt
rēxēre for rēxērunt

(*e*) Perfect Infinitive Active

e.g. laud**āsse** for laudāvisse
aud**īsse** for audīvisse

N.B. (*c*) (*e*) only occur in Verbs which have a **-v** in their **Perfect Stem.**

(*f*) In the Fourth Conjugation the **-v** of the **Perfect Stem** is often omitted.

e.g. audi**erim** for audīverim
sci**it** for scīvit

67. *Defective Verbs*

ōdī, *I hate* **meminī,** *I remember* **nōvī,** *I know*	are found only in the **Perfect** tenses.

Observe the rule,
Latin Perfect = English Present
Latin Pluperfect = English Past
Latin Future Perfect = English Future

ōdī, *I hate*	**meminī,** *I remember*	**nōvī,** *I know*
ōderam, *I hated*	**memineram,** *I remembered*	**nōveram,** *I knew*
ōderō, *I shall hate*	**meminerō,** *I shall remember*	**nōverō,** *I shall know*

ōdisse, *to hate*
meminisse, *to remember*
nōvisse, *to know*

Similarly with the Subjunctive Mood

ōderim **meminerim** **nōverim**	= Present Subjunctive
ōdissem **meminissem** **nōvissem**	= Imperfect or Past Subjunctive

N.B. The Imperative of **memini** is **mementō**
mementōte

XII. NUMBERS

68.

	DISTRIBUTIVES (*one each*, etc.)	ADVERBS (*once*, *twice*, etc.)
1	singul**ī-ae-a**	semel
2	bīn**ī**	bis
3	tern**ī**, trīn**ī**	ter
4	quatern**ī**	quater
5	quīn**ī**	quīnqu**iēs**
6	sēn**ī**	sex**iēs**
7	septēn**ī**	sept**iēs**
8	octōn**ī**	oct**iēs**
9	novēn**ī**	nov**iēs**
10	dēn**ī**	dec**iēs**
11	ūndēn**ī**	ūndec**iēs**
12	duodēn**ī**	duodec**iēs**
13	tern**ī** den**ī**	terdec**iēs**
14	quatern**ī** dēn**ī**	quater dec**iēs**
15	quīn**ī** dēni	quīndec**iēs**
16	sēn**ī** dēn**ī**	sēdec**iēs**
17	septēn**ī** dēn**ī**	sept**iēs** dec**iēs**
18	duodēvīcēn**ī**	duodēvīc**iēs**
19	ūndēvīcēn**ī**	ūndēvīc**iēs**
20	vīcēn**ī**	vīc**iēs**
30	trīcēn**ī**	trīc**iēs**
40	quadrāgēn**ī**	quadrāg**iēs**
50	quīnquāgēn**ī**	quīnquāg**iēs**
60	sexāgēn**ī**	sexāg**iēs**
70	septuāgēn**ī**	septuāg**iēs**
80	octōgēn**ī**	octōg**iēs**
90	nōnāgēn**ī**	nōnāg**iēs**
100	centēn**ī**	cent**iēs**
200	ducēn**ī**	ducent**iēs**
300	trecēn**ī**	trecent**iēs**
400	quadringēn**ī**	quadringent**iēs**
500	quīngēn**ī**	quīngent**iēs**
600	sēscēn**ī**	sescent**iēs**

700	septingēnī	septingentiēs
800	octingēnī	octingentiēs
900	nōngēnī	nōngentiēs
1000	singula mīlia	mīliēs

N.B. **(i)** Distinguish the use of the **Cardinal** and **Distributive.**

e.g. **Tria** māla puerīs dedit, *he gave the boys three apples.*
Terna māla puerīs dedit, *he gave the boys three apples each.*

(ii) Distributives are used instead of Cardinals with Nouns **Plural** in form but **Singular** in meaning.

e.g. **Bīna** castra, *two camps*
Bis **bīna** sunt quattuor, $2 \times 2 = 4$
Trīnae litterae, *three letters*

(iii) Fractions of the type $\frac{n-1}{n}$ are expressed thus,

sex partēs $= \frac{6}{7}$

trēs partēs $= \frac{3}{4}$

(iv) 1,000,000 is **deciēs centēna mīlia,** i.e. $10 \times 100{,}000$
Centēna mīlia is often omitted especially in sums of money.

e.g. Vīciēs sēstertium = vīciēs **centēna mīlia** sēstertium
$= 20 \times 100{,}000$
$= 2{,}000{,}000$ *sesterces*

(v) prīmum, *for the first time*
iterum, *for the second time*
postrēmum, *for the last time*

In arguments, prīmum, *firstly*
deinde, *secondly*
postrēmo / dēnique, *finally*

Essential Syntax

XIII. NOUNS

69. *Nominative Case*

The Nominative is used to indicate the **Subject** of the Verb.

e.g. **Puer** pilam iacit. *The boy throws the ball.*

70. *Vocative Case*

The Vocative is used **to address** a person and always has the **same** ending as the Nominative except in the Singular of **-us** and **-ius Nouns of the Second Declension.**

e.g. Festīnā domum, **serve.** *Hurry home, slave.*

71. *Accusative Case*

(*a*) The Accusative is used to indicate the **Direct Object** of the Verb.

e.g. Mīles **hastam** tenet. *The soldier holds his spear.*

(*b*) The Accusative is used in **Exclamations.**

e.g. O **mē miserum**! *Dear me!*
Quantam impudentiam! *What great impudence!*

(*c*) The Accusative Neuter Singular of an **Adjective** or a **Pronoun** may be used as an **Adverb.**

e.g. **Nihil** assentior. *I do not agree at all* (lit. *in no way do I agree*).
Quid erravērunt? *In what respect have they erred?*

72. *Genitive Case*

(*a*) The Genitive is used to indicate **Possession.**

e.g. Mīlitēs **rēgis** victī sunt. *The* {*soldiers of the king* / *king's soldiers*} *were defeated.*

(*b*) The Genitive is used to indicate that only a **Part** or **Some** of the whole is involved, after a **Neuter Adjective, Pronoun** or **Adverb.**

e.g. nihil	**pecūniae**	*no*	*money*
aliquid		*some*	
nimis		*too much*	
parum		*too little*	
satis		*enough*	
plūs		*more*	
minus		*less*	
tantum		*so much*	
quantum		*how much*	

N.B. Nostrum and **vestrum** are the Genitive Plurals of **ego** and **tū** which indicate **some** or **part.**

e.g. Quis **vestrum**? *Who of you?*
but Omnēs **nōs.** *All of us.*

(*c*) The Genitive is used, always with an **Adjective,** to indicate an **Internal Quality.**

e.g. Fēmina **magnae virtūtis.** *A woman of great courage.*

The Genitive tends to be used for internal or permanent qualities, the Ablative for external ones, vid. sec. 74 (*e*).

(*d*) The Genitive is used to indicate **Value** after, **aestimō, habeō, dūcō, faciō,** *value.*
There are twelve common expressions of **Value.**

magnī, *greatly*	**plūris**	**plūrimī**
parvī, *at a little*	**minōris**	**minimī**
tantī, *at so much*	**quantī**	**tantulī,** *at so little*
nihilī, *at nothing*	**naucī,** *at a nut*	**floccī,** *at a straw*

e.g. Librōs **plūris** quam dīvitiās aestimābat. *He valued his books more highly than his wealth.*

Magnī mātrem habēbās. *You cared a lot for your mother.*
Floccī magistrum nōn facimus. *We do not care a straw for the teacher.*

(*e*) **Tantī, quantī, plūris, minōris** are used with the verbs **emō,** *buy* and **vendō,** *sell* to express **Price.** Vid. sec. 74 (*f*)

e.g. **Quantī** domum ēmistī? {*How much did you pay for the house? / What did the house cost you?*}

(*f*) The Genitive is used after the following Adjectives.

cupidus, *desirous of*
avidus, *eager for*
studiōsus, *devoted to*
memor, *mindful of*
immemor, *heedless of*
similis, *like*
perītus, *skilled in*
imperītus, *unskilled in*
īnsuētus, *unaccustomed to*
expers, *without a share in*
particeps, *sharing in*
dissimilis, *unlike*

Also the Present Participles

amāns, *devoted to*
patiēns, *enduring of, inured to*

(*g*) The Genitive is used with the Verbs, **accūsō,** *accuse,* **damnō,** *condemn,* **absolvō,** *acquit* to indicate the **Charge** or **Punishment.**

e.g. **Perfidiae** accūsātus est. *He was accused of treachery.*
Nōs **capitis** damnābunt. *They will condemn us to death.*

73. *Dative Case*

(*a*) The Dative is used to indicate the **Indirect Object** of the Verb, often shown in English by **to** and **for.**

e.g. Gladium **mihi** dedit. *He gave the sword **to** me.*

(*b*) The Dative can indicate **Possession.**

e.g. **Nōbīs** canis est. *We have a dog.*

(*c*) The Dative can indicate **Purpose** and is followed by a second Dative of the **Person** or **Thing.** It is known as a **Predicative Dative.**

auxiliō esse, *to help*	**dēdecorī esse,** *to be a disgrace to*
auxiliō venīre, *to come to the help of*	**praesidiō esse,** *to guard*
auxiliō mittere, *to send to the help of*	**odiō esse,** *to be hated by*
beneficiō esse, *to be of advantage to*	**impedīmentō esse,** *to be a hindrance to*
ūsuī esse, *to be of use to*	**exemplō esse,** *to be an example*

e.g. Equitēs **peditibus auxiliō** mīsērunt. *They sent the cavalry to the help of the infantry.*
Odiō eīs eram. *I was hated by them.*

(*d*) The Dative is used after the following Adjectives

benignus, *kind*	**necessārius,** *necessary*
difficilis, *difficult*	**ūtilis,** *useful*
facilis, *easy*	**inūtilis,** *useless*
grātus, *pleasing*	**par,** *equal to*
idōneus, *suitable*	**impar,** *unequal*

74. *Ablative Case*

(*a*) The Ablative is used with **ā(b)** after a Passive Verb to indicate the **Agent.**

e.g. **Ā magistrō** laudātus sum. *I was praised by the teacher.*

(*b*) The Ablative is used **without** a preposition after an Active or Passive Verb to indicate the **Instrument** used.

e.g. **Hastā** vulnerātus est. *He was wounded by a spear.*

(*c*) The Ablative is used to indicate **How** an action is performed.

e.g. **Summā** cum **celeritāte** Rōmam vēnērunt. *They came to Rome with all speed.*

N.B. If there is no **Adjective** present, **cum** is generally used. If there is an **Adjective** present, **cum** is optional.

e.g. **cum** cūrā. *With care.*
magnā (**cum**) cūrā. *With great care.*

(*d*) The Ablative is used **without** a preposition to indicate **Why** an action takes place.

e.g. **Fame** periērunt. *They died of hunger.*
Mīles **īgnāviā** damnātus est. *The soldier was condemned because of his cowardice.*

(*e*) The Ablative is used with an **Adjective** to describe an **External** or **Physical Feature,** vid. sec. 72 (*c*).

e.g. Vir **nigrā barbā.** *A man with a black beard.*
Nāvis **altō mālō.** *A ship with a high mast.*

(*f*) The Ablative is used after the Verbs, **emō,** *buy* and **vendō,** *sell* to express **Price,** vid. sec. 72 (*e*).

e.g. **Duōbus mīlibus** sēstertium domum ēmit. *He bought the house for two thousand sesterces.*
Vīlī equum vendidit. *He sold the horse cheaply.*

(*g*) The Ablative can be used after a **Comparative** to replace **quam** with a **Nominative** or **Accusative.**

e.g. Tu fortior **mē** es. *You are braver than I.*

(*h*) The Ablative is used after the following **Adjectives.**

dīgnus, *worthy of*
indīgnus, *unworthy of*
contentus, *content with*
orbus, *bereft of*
frētus, *relying on*
praeditus, *endowed with*
ortus, *descended from*
vacuus, *empty of*

XIV. ADJECTIVES

75. (*a*) An Adjective tells us something about a Noun or Pronoun and so agrees with it in **Case, Number** and **Gender.**

e.g. Pōns **maximus** factus est. *A very large bridge was built.*
Puellae erant **pulchrae.** *The girls were beautiful.*
In urbe **parvā.** *In a small city.*

(*b*) If an Adjective describes persons of different sex, it generally becomes **Masculine** and **Plural.**

e.g. Puer et puella **bonī** sunt. *The boy and girl are good.*

(*c*) If an Adjective describes things of different gender, it generally becomes **Neuter** and **Plural.**

e.g. Domus et templum erant **pulchra.** *The house and temple were beautiful.*

N.B. In (*b*) and (*c*) the Adjective may agree with the **nearest** Noun.

e.g. Laudātus est pater et māter. *My father and mother were praised.*

76. The English Nouns, *top of*, *bottom of*, etc. are replaced by **Adjectives** in Latin.

summus, *top of*	**reliquus,** *rest of*
medius, *middle of*	**tōtus,** *whole of*
īmus, *bottom of*	**extrēmus,** *edge of*
	cēterī, *the rest of*

e.g. Ad **summum** collem pervēnit. *He reached the top of the hill.*
Cum **reliquō** exercitū prōgressus est. *He advanced with the rest of the army.*

XV. PRONOUNS

77. *Personal Pronouns*

(*a*) *I*, *you*, etc. are normally not expressed in Latin but indicated by the **ending** of the Verb. **Ego, tū,** etc. are used for **emphasis.**

e.g. **Ego** rūs īvī, **tū** domī manēbās. *I went to the country, you stayed at home.*

(*b*) Latin is not a polite language: **ego** is written before **tū,** and **tū** before **is.**

e.g. **Ego** et **tū** aderāmus. *You and I were present.*
Tū et **is** ā magistrō culpātī estis. *He and you were blamed by the teacher.*

N.B. A **First and Second Person Subject** makes the Verb **First Plural.**

A **Second and Third Person Subject** makes the Verb **Second Plural.**

78. *Relative Pronouns.*

The Relative agrees with its **Antecedent** in **Number, Person** and **Gender,** but its **Case** is decided by its **position** in its **own clause.**

e.g. Linter **quam** vīdimus est vestra. *The boat which we saw is yours.*

Puella **cūius** pila āmissa erat flēbat. *The girl whose ball had been lost was weeping.*

Vōs, **quī** adestis, gaudēre dēbētis. *You who are here should rejoice.*

XVI. COMPARATIVES AND SUPERLATIVES

79. *Comparatives*

(*a*) When comparing one person or thing with another, Latin uses the word **quam** with the same case **after** it as **before** it.

e.g. Poēta est māior **quam** agricola. *The poet is bigger than the farmer.*

Puellam stultiōrem **quam** puerum vocāvit. *He called the girl more stupid than the boy.*

N.B. Quam with a **Nominative** or **Accusative** may be replaced by the **Ablative,** vid. sec. 74 (*g*).

(*b*) If two Adjectives are compared, **both** must be **Comparatives.**

e.g. Mīles est stultior quam **ignāvior.** *The soldier is more stupid than lazy.*

(*c*) In English a phrase such as **that of** frequently occurs after a Comparative, in Latin it is **not** translated.

e.g. Meus canis est māior quam **Publiī.** *My dog is bigger than that of Publius.*

(*d*) **Quam** is omitted after **plūs, amplius** and **minus.**

e.g. **Plūs** septuāgintā mīlitēs occīsī sunt. *More than seventy soldiers were killed.*

(*e*) The Comparative can also have the meanings, *rather, too, quite.*

e.g. Ille est pulchrior. *That man is* {*rather* / *quite* / *too*} *handsome.*

80. *Superlatives*

(*a*) The Superlatives can also have the meanings, *very*, *extremely*.

e.g. Puella erat tardissima. *The girl was* {*very* / *extremely*} *slow*.

(*b*) **Quam** with the Superlative means, *as . . . as possible*.

e.g. **Quam celerrimē** cucurrērunt. *They ran as quickly as possible*.

(*c*) The Superlative is often used with a person's name thus, Caesar vir **fortissimus.** *The brave Caesar*.

XVII. VERBS

81. *Present Tense*

(*a*) The Present denotes what is going on **now** or what **is.**

e.g. Canis **currit.** *The dog runs, is running, does run*.
Canis **est** ferōx. *The dog is fierce*.

(*b*) The Present denotes an action begun in the **past** and still going on **now,** usually with the Adverbs **iam, iam diū, dūdum, prīdem.**

e.g. Trēs iam hōrās **adsum.** *I have been here for three hours* (*and still am here*).

Iam {diū / dūdum / prīdem} in murō **sedeō.** *I have long been sitting on the wall* (*and still am sitting*).

(*c*) The Present is frequently used in Latin instead of the Perfect to make a narrative more vivid and exciting for the reader.

e.g. Metellus ab Zamā **discēdit,** et in hīs urbibus, quae ad sē dēfēcerant, praesidia **impōnit;** cēterum exercitum in Numidiā **collocat.**

Metellus left Zama and put garrisons in those towns which had revolted to him; the rest of the army he stationed in Numidia.

82. *Future Tense*

The Future denotes what is **going** to happen or what will **be.**

e.g. Ad tē **scrībam.** *I shall write to you.*
Epistula longa **erit.** *The letter will be long.*

83. *Imperfect Tense*

(*a*) The Imperfect denotes what **went on** or what **was for a long time.**

e.g. Puer **lacrimābat** et īnfēlīx **erat.** *The boy was crying and was unhappy.*

(*b*) The Imperfect denotes a **repeated action** in the **past.**

e.g. Prīmā lūce **surgēbat.** *He used to get up at dawn.*

(*c*) The Imperfect denotes an **attempted action** in the **past.**

e.g. Puer arborem **ascendēbat.** *The boy tried to climb the tree.*

(*d*) The Imperfect denotes an action begun in the **past** and **still continuing** at the time mentioned, usually with Adverbs, **iam, iam diū, dūdum, pridem**

e.g. Trēs iam hōrās **aderam.** *I had been present for three hours (and still was present).*

Iam {diū / dūdum / prīdem} in murō **sedēbam.** *I had long been sitting on the wall (and still was sitting).*

84. *Perfect Tense*

(*a*) The Perfect denotes a **'once'** action in the past, i.e. without **have.**

e.g. **Vēnī, vīdī, vīcī.** *I came, I saw, I conquered.*

(*b*) The Perfect denotes the **present** result of a **past** action, i.e. with **have.**

e.g. Pontem **fēcērunt.** *They have built the bridge.*

85. *Future Perfect Tense*

The Future Perfect denotes an action which will take place **before** another action in the **future.** In Latin it occurs most commonly in **Subordinate Clauses** where English uses a Present.

e.g. Sī **redieris,** poenās dabis. *If you return, you will be punished.*
Cum Rōmam **vēnerit,** Cicerōnem audiet. *When he comes to Rome, he will listen to Cicero.*

86. *Pluperfect Tense*

The Pluperfect denotes an action already completed **before** another action in the **past.**

e.g. Rēgem **occīderant** priusquam pervēnimus. *They had killed the king before we arrived.*

87. *The Infinitive*

The Infinitive which is really a **Noun** can act as **Subject** or **Object.**

(*a*) As Subject

e.g. **Natāre** est facile. {*To swim* / *Swimming*} *is easy.*

(*b*) As Object

e.g. Latīnē **scrībere** possum. *I can write Latin.*
Natāre sciō. *I know how to swim.*

N.B. The following Verbs take the Infinitive as Object.

volō, *wish, be willing*	**prohibeō,** *prevent*
nōlō, *be unwilling*	**audeō,** *dare*
mālō, *prefer*	**cōnor,** *try*
possum, *be able, can*	**dēsinō,** *cease*
dēbeō, *ought*	{**dubitō** / **cūnctor**} *hesitate*
{**statuō** / **cōnstituō**} *decide*	
cupiō, *desire*	**soleō,** *be accustomed to*
sinō, *allow*	**sciō,** *know*
cōgō, *compel*	**coepī,** *began*

N.B. (i) Possum, dēbeō are **never** followed by a Perfect Infinitive as in English.

e.g. **Venīre** {poterat. / dēbuit.} *He* {*could have come.* / *ought to have come.*}

(ii) Coepī if followed by a **Passive Infinitive** becomes **Passive** itself.

e.g. Urbs oppugnārī **coepta est.** *The city began to be attacked.*

(*c*) In Latin the **Present Infinitive** can be used instead of a **Perfect Indicative** to denote a quick moving vivid narrative and is known as the **Historic Infinitive.**

e.g. Verrēs **minitārī** eī, **vōciferārī,** lacrimās interdum vix **tenēre.**

Verres uttered threats against him, shouted aloud, at times could hardly restrain his tears.

88. *Participles*

Present Participle

(*a*) The Present Participle denotes an action going on at the **same time** as the **Main Verb** and is often equivalent to a **'while'** clause.

e.g. **Rediēns** domum, lupum vīdit.

{*Returning home* / *While he was returning home*} *he saw a wolf.*

Puerōs **aufugientēs** animadvertit.

He noticed the boys {*running away.* / *while they were running away.*}

(*b*) In Latin a Present Participle is not used in the **Nominative Case** if there is any suggestion of **Cause, cum** is used with a **Present** or **Imperfect Subjunctive.**

e.g. **Cum** magistrum **timēret,** puer tacēbat.

{*Fearing the teacher* / *Since he feared the teacher*} *the boy kept silent.*

(*c*) A Present Participle can be used to translate such **Nouns** as, *audience*, *bystanders*, etc.

e.g. Clāmōrēs **audientium.** *The shouts of the audience.*

Adstantēs vītāvit. *He avoided the bystanders.*

N.B. In Latin a Present Participle by **itself** can often be translated by a **Relative Clause.**

e.g. **Pugnantēs** spectābam. *I watched those who were fighting.*

89. *Perfect Participle*

(*a*) The Perfect Participle denotes an action finished **before** that of the **Main Verb.**

e.g. Puerī **laudātī** ā cōnsule gaudēbant.

The boys {*having been praised* / *praised*} *by the consul were happy.*

(*b*) The Perfect Participle of Deponent Verb is **Active** in meaning.

e.g. **Regressī** ad castra cubitum īvērunt.

{*Having returned* / *Returning*} *to the camp they went to bed.*

N.B. English often uses a Present Participle to denote an action finished **before** that of the Main Verb, but Latin being more precise uses the correct Participle, the **Perfect.**

(*c*) Latin often uses a **Perfect Participle** in agreement with a **Noun** in the **Accusative Case** and **one** Main Verb where English uses two Verbs joined by **and.**

e.g. Faelis mūrem **captum** ēdit. *The cat caught the mouse and ate it.*

(*d*) For Ablative Absolute vid. sec. 103.

90. *Future Participle*

(*a*) The Future Participle denotes an action that is **about to** or **going to take place.**

e.g. Arborem **cāsūram** spectābam.

I watched the tree {*about to fall.* / *going to fall.* / *on the point of falling.*}

(*b*) The Future Participle is often used with **sum** or **eram** to denote **intention** or **likelihood.**

e.g. **Reditūrī** sunt. *They are* {*going to* / *likely to* / *intending to*} *return.*

Discessūrī erant. *They were on the* {*point* / *verge*} *of leaving.*

91. In Latin the following Verbs put their **Object** into the **Dative.**

(*a*) FIRST CONJUGATION

imperō, *order*
appropinquō, *approach*
obtemperō, *obey*
vacō, *have leisure for*

SECOND CONJUGATION

displiceō, *displease*
faveō, *favour*
indulgeō, *indulge in*
invideō, *envy*
medeor, *heal*
noceō, *harm*
pāreō, *obey*
persuādeō, *persuade*
placeō, *please*
studeō, *study*
suādeō, *persuade*

THIRD CONJUGATION

cōnfīdō, fīdō, *trust*
cōnsulō, *consult the interest of.*
crēdō, *believe*
diffīdō, *distrust*
īgnōscō, *pardon*
īrāscor, *be angry with*
nūbō, *marry*
obsistō, obstō, *obstruct*
occurrō, *meet*
parcō, *spare*
resistō, *resist*
serviō, *serve, play the slave to*
subveniō, *help*
succurrō, *help*

N.B. (i) crēdō is followed by the **Dative** of **Person,** but **Accusative** of a **Neuter Pronoun** (to avoid ambiguity).

e.g. **Eī** crēdēbāmus. *We believed him.*
Id crēdēbāmus. *We believed that.*

(ii) cōnsulō + Accusative means *consult*
cōnsulō + Dative means *consult the interests of*
cōnsulō + dē + Ablative means *consult about*

(*b*) In the **Passive** these Verbs must be used **Impersonally,** i.e. **it** becomes the **Subject** and the English Subject goes into the **Dative.**

e.g. **Eī** crēditur. *He is believed.*
Tibi parsum est. *You were spared.*

92. In Latin the following Verbs put their **Objects** into the **Genitive.**

meminī, *I remember*
oblīvīscor, *I forget*
misereor, *I pity*

N.B. meminī and **oblīvīscor** take the **Genitive** of **Person** and the **Accusative** or **Genitive** of **Thing,** but if the **Object** is a **Neuter Pronoun,** the **Accusative** must be used.

e.g. **Tuī** meminī sed {**tuum nōmen** / **tuī nōminis**} oblīvīscor.

I remember you, but forget your name.
But, mementō **hōc.** *Remember this.*

93. In Latin the following Verbs put their **Objects** into the **Ablative.**

ūtor, *use* — **vescor,** *feed on*
abūtor, *use up* — **careō,** *lack* (usually a luxury)
fruor, *enjoy* — **egeō,** *need* (an essential)
fungor, *perform* — **opus est,** *there is need of*
potior, *gain control of*

N.B. Opus est takes the **Dative** of **Subject, Ablative** of **Thing Needed.**

e.g. **Tibi pecūniā** opus erit. *You will need money.*

94. In Latin there are numerous Verbs which are used **Impersonally,** i.e. the **Subject** is **it** and the Verb if Indicative or Subjunctive is always **Third Person Singular.**

(*a*) The following Verbs take the **Accusative** of **Person** and are followed by the **Present Infinitive.**

mē decet, *it becomes me*
mē dēdecet, *it ill becomes me*
mē oportet, *it behoves me, I ought to*

N.B. Oportet can only be followed by a **Present Infinitive.**

e.g. Tē **venīre** oportuit. *You should have come.*

(*b*) The following Verbs take the **Dative** of the **Subject** and are followed by a **Present Infinitive.**

mihi vidētur, *it seems good to me, I am resolved*
mihi placet, *it pleases me, I am resolved*
mihi licet, *it is allowed to me, I may*
mihi libet, *it pleases me, I like*

e.g. **Eī redīre** licuit. *He was allowed to return.*

(*c*) The following Verbs take the **Accusative** of the **Subject** and **Genitive** of the **Cause.**

mē miseret, *I pity, feel sorry for*
mē paenitet, *I repent of*
mē piget, *I am vexed with*
mē pudet, *I am ashamed of*
mē taedet, *I am tired of*

e.g. **Nōs senis** miserēbat. *We felt sorry for the old man.*

N.B. (i) A **Prohibition** is expressed by **ne+Present Subjunctive.**

e.g. **Nē** tē meī **pudeat.** *Don't be ashamed of me.*

(ii) If the **Object** is a **Neuter Pronoun,** it goes into the **Nominative.**

e.g. **Hōc** mē paenitēbit. *I shall repent of this.*

(iii) These Verbs may be followed by an **Infinitive.**

e.g. **Discessisse** domō mē nōn paenitet. *I do not regret having left home.*

(Note that here, **discessisse** is really **Subject,** i.e. *To have left home does not repent me.*)

(*d*) Many **Intransitive Verbs** are used **Impersonally** in the **Passive.**

e.g. Concursum est. *There was a rush.*
Ad Britanniam ventum est. *Britain was reached.*
Diū ac ācriter pugnātum est. *There was a long and fierce battle.*

(*e*) **Interest,** *it is of importance to,* is followed by a **Genitive** of the **Person** except **meā, tuā, nostrā, vestrā.**

e.g. {**Rōmānōrum** / **Nostrā**} interesat. *It was of importance to* {*the Romans.* / *us.*}

N.B. (i) Interest may be used with a **Genitive of Value,** an **Adverb,** or the **Neuter Singular** of an **Adjective** used as an **Adverb.**

e.g. {**Magnī** / **Magnopere** / **Multum**} meā intererit. *It will be of great importance to me.*

(ii) Interest may be followed by

(*a*) **Plain Infinitive**

(*b*) **Accusative and Infinitive**

(*c*) **Explanatory ut + Subjunctive**

(*d*) **Indirect Question**

e.g. Plūrimī interest {collem **capere.** / **eōs** collem **capere.** / **ut** collem **capiant.**}

It is of the greatest importance {*to capture the hill.* / *that they should capture the hill.*}

Nostrā nōn interest **utrum canās necne.**

It is immaterial to us whether you sing or not.

(*f*) **Rēfert,** *it concerns, is of importance to,* is followed only by **meā, tuā, nostrā, vestrā.**

e.g. {Nōn / Nihil} **meā** rēfert. *It makes no difference to me.*

(*g*) Latin has a small group of impersonal **Weather Verbs.**

pluit, *it rains*
ningit, *it snows*
tonat, *it thunders*
fulgurat, *there is lightning*

95. *Gerund*

The Gerund is a **Verbal Noun** (vid. sec. 64) used as follows

(*a*) In the **Accusative** with **ad** to express **Purpose.**

e.g. **Ad dīripiendum** vēnērunt. *They came to plunder.*

(*b*) In the **Genitive** after another Noun and with **causa** to express **Purpose.**

e.g. Ars **canendī.** *The art of singing.*
Dīripiendī causa vēnērunt. *They came to plunder.*

(*c*) In the **Ablative** to express **Instrument** and with a **Preposition.**

e.g. **In dormiendō** tempus terēbant. *They wasted time in sleeping.*
Audiendō discēs. *You will learn by listening.*

96. *Gerundive*

The Gerundive is a **Verbal Adjective Passive** in meaning – i.e. *requiring to be* – and is used as follows.

(*a*) To replace the **Gerund** when it has an **Object.**

e.g. Lēgātiōnibus **mittendīs.** *By sending embassies.*
Ad urbem **dīripiendam** / Urbis **dīripiendae** causa. } *To plunder the city.*

N.B. The Gerund is retained when
(i) the Verb takes the **Dative**
(ii) the **Object** is a **Neuter Pronoun**

(*b*) To express **Obligation,** i.e. English, *must, have to.* The Latin sentence is in the **Passive** with the **Agent** in the **Dative.**

e.g. Puer **magistrō laudandus** est.
Lit. *The boy is requiring to be praised by the teacher.*
i.e. *The teacher must praise the boy.*
Puellae **tibi monendae** erant.
Lit. *The girls were requiring to be warned by you.*
i.e. *You had to warn the girls.*

N.B. (i) The Gerundive is used **Impersonally** if the Verb is **Intransitive.**

(ii) The Gerundive is used **Impersonally** if the Verb takes the **Dative** and the **Agent** is expressed by **ā(b)** with the **Ablative.**

e.g. Nōbīs **festīnandum** erit. *We shall have to hurry.*
Cōnsulī **ā mīlitibus pārendum** est. *The soldiers must obey the consul.*

(*c*) In the **Accusative** after the Verb **cūrō,** *I have something done.*

e.g. Caesar pontem **faciendum** in flūmine cūrāvit.
Caesar had a bridge built across the river.

XVIII. TIME, PLACE AND SPACE

97. *Time*

(*a*) Time **How Long** goes into the **Accusative Case. No Preposition.** English indicates Time How Long by **for** or by simply stating the length of time.

e.g. **Trēs mēnsēs** rēgnābat. *He ruled (for) three months.*

(*b*) **All other time phrases** go into the **Ablative Case. No Preposition.** English uses such Prepositions as **in, within, at, on, during.**

e.g. { **Tribus diēbus** / **Prīmā lūce** / **Tertiō diē** / **Aestāte** } redībunt. *They will return* { *in three days.* / *at dawn.* / *on the third day.* / *during the summer.* }

N.B.	**decem ante annīs.**	*Ten years before.*
	decem post annīs.	*Ten years after.*
	abhinc annōs decem.	*Ten years ago.*

98. *Place*

(*a*) **To, from, in** a place are expressed by the Prepositions **ad, ē(x), ā(b), in** except with names of **Towns,** and the Nouns, **domus, rūs** and **humus.**

e.g. { **Ad** / **In** } castra cucurrit. *He ran* { *to* / *into* } *the camp.*

{ **Ē** / **Ā** } castrīs fūgit. *He fled* { *out of* / *from* } *the camp.*

In castrīs manēbat. *He remained in the camp.*

But Rōmam īvit. *He went to Rome.*

Londīniō vēnit. *He came from London.*

N.B. **(i)** The following table

	TO	FROM	AT/IN/ON
home	dom**um**	dom**ō**	dom**ī**
country	rūs	rūr**e**	rūr**ī**
ground	ad, in hum**um**	hum**ō**	hum**ī**

(ii) Prepositions must be used with the names of **Countries.**

e.g. **Ad** Britanniam. *To Britain.*
Ex Hispaniā. *From Spain.*

(*b*) To translate **in** or **at** with the name of a town, the **Genitive Singular** is used if the name of the town is **Singular** and belongs to the **First** or **Second Declension.** Otherwise the **Dative Case** is used. This is known as the **Locative Case.**

	TO	FROM	IN/AT
Rome	Rōm**am**	Rōm**ā**	Rōm**ae**
Athens	Athēn**ās**	Athēn**īs**	Athēn**īs**
London	Londīn**ium**	Londīn**iō**	Londīn**iī**
Carthage	Carthāgin**em**	Carthāgin**e**	Carthāgin**ī**
Naples	Neāpol**im**	Neāpol**ī**	Neāpol**ī**
Cadiz	Gad**ēs**	Gad**ibus**	Gad**ibus**

99. *Space*

All **Measurement** goes into the **Accusative Case. No Preposition.**

e.g. **Decem mīlia passuum** prōgressī sumus.
We advanced ten miles.
Flūmen **centum pedēs** lātum.
A river one hundred feet broad.

XIX. SIMPLE CONSTRUCTIONS

100. *Direct Question*

(*a*) In Latin a **Direct Question** can be expressed by

(i) an **Interrogative** word.
(ii) **-ne,** when no definite answer is expected.
(iii) **Nōnne,** when the answer **Yes** is expected.
(iv) **Num,** when the answer **No** is expected.

e.g. **Quis** es? **Quid** fēcistī? **Quandō** discēdēs?
Who are you? What have you done? When will you leave?
Potes**ne** hōc intellegere?
Can you understand this?
Nōnne hōc intellegis?
{Surely *you understand this?*
{*You understand this,* don't you*?*
{Don't *you understand this?*
Num hōc intellegis?
{Surely *you do* not *understand this?*
{*You* don't *understand this,* do you*?*

N.B. **–ne** is added to the **first** word, but not to a preposition.

(*b*) In Latin a **Double Direct Question** can be expressed by

(i) **Utrum . . . an (annōn)**
(ii) **-ne . . . an (annōn)**
(iii) **— . . . an (annōn)**

e.g. {**Utrum** Londīniī **an** Lutētiae manēbis?
{Londīniī**ne** manēbis **an** Lutētiae?
{Londīniī **an** Lutētiae manēbis?
(Whether) will you remain in London or Paris?
{**Utrum** vīnum amās **annōn?**
{Vīnum**ne** amās **annōn?**
Do you like wine or not?

101. *Direct Commands and Prohibitions*

Latin expresses a Direct Command in the Second Person by using the **Imperative.** A Command in the First or Third Person is expressed by the **Present Subjunctive.** A Prohibition in the Second Person is expressed by **nōlī(te)** with the **Present Infinitive.** A Prohibition in the First or Third Person is expressed by **nē** with the **Present Subjunctive.** Thus in table form

	+ VE	− VE
First Person	**Present Subjunctive**	**Nē + Present Subjunctive**
Second Person	**Present Imperative**	**Nōlī(te) + Present Infinitive**
Third Person	**Present Subjunctive**	**Nē + Present Subjunctive**

e.g. **Veniāmus.** *Let us come.*
Manē. *Stay.*
Redeant. *Let them return.*
Nē redeāmus. *Let us not return.*
Nōlī manēre. *Don't stay.*

N.B. Nē + Perfect Subjunctive may be used instead of **nōlī.**

e.g. **Nē secūtus sīs.** *Don't follow.*

102. *Wishes*

In Latin the **Subjunctive** is used to express a **Wish** with **utinam,** negative **utinam nē.**

(*a*) A **Wish** for the **Future** is expressed by **utinam + Present Subjunctive.**

e.g. **Utinam** falsus vātēs **sim.** *O that I may be a false prophet.*

(*b*) A **Wish** for the **Present** is expressed by **utinam + Imperfect Subjunctive.**

e.g. **Utinam nē adessēs.** *Would that you were not here.*

(*c*) A **Wish** for the **Past** is expressed by **utinam + Pluperfect Subjunctive.**

e.g. **Utinam** Rōmae **mānsissēs.**
{*Would that* / *If only*} *you had stayed in Rome.*

XX. SUBORDINATE CONSTRUCTIONS

103. *Ablative Absolute*

(*a*) In Latin a **Noun** or **Pronoun** in the **Ablative Case** is often used with a **Participle** in agreement to express the idea of **Time, Cause,** and **Concession.** This is known as an **Ablative Absolute.** The **Noun** or **Pronoun** and **Participle** have no **grammatical** connection with the rest of the sentence.

e.g. **Urbe incēnsā,** Rōmānī sē rēcēpērunt.

When / *After* / *Since* / *Although* } *the city had been burned, the Romans retreated.*

(*b*) The **Perfect Participle** is the Participle most commonly found in this construction, but the **Present Participle** is used very often to express the idea of **Time.** The Future Participle rarely occurs in an Ablative Absolute.

e.g. **Mē redeunte,** turris incēnsa est.
While I was returning, the tower was burned.

N.B. An Ablative Absolute can only be used if the **Participle** agrees with neither the **Subject** nor the **Object** of the **Main Verb.**

(*c*) As the Verb **to be** does not have a Present Participle, it is possible to have an Ablative Absolute consisting of **Two Nouns** or a **Noun** and an **Adjective** with the Participle 'being' understood.

e.g. **Numā rēge,** lit. *Numa being king, in the reign of Numa.*

Thus

Caesare duce, *under the leadership of Caesar*
meā mātre vīvā, *in my mother's lifetime*
mē īnsciō, *without my knowledge*
tē auctōre, *at your instigation*
adversō flūmine, *upstream*
secundō flūmine, *downstream*
nōbīs invītīs, *against our will*
Cicerōne cōnsule, *in the consulship of Cicero*

104. *Indirect Statement*

(*a*) Veniam. *I shall come,* is a Direct Statement. Dīxī **mē ventūrum esse.** *I said that I would come,* is an **Indirect**

Statement. Thus an **Indirect Statement** is a **Noun Clause** objective after Verbs of **saying, thinking, believing, etc.** In Latin the **Subject** of the **Noun Clause** goes into the **Accusative,** the **Verb** of the **Noun Clause** goes into the **Infinitive.**

e.g. Sciēbāmus **urbem captam esse.**
We knew the city had been captured.

The following table shows how to translate the **Infinitive.**

Present Infinitive = *is, was, were.*
Perfect Infinitive = *have, has, had.*
Future Infinitive = *will, would.*

e.g. Putāmus puellam { **venīre.** / **vēnisse.** / **ventūram esse.** }

We think (that) the girl { *is coming.* / *has come.* / *will come.* }

Putābāmus puellam { **venīre.** / **vēnisse.** / **ventūram esse.** }

We thought (that) the girl { *was coming.* / *had come.* / *would come.* }

N.B. When translating into Latin beware of **was, were** after a **Present Tense** when a **Perfect Infinitive** is required.

e.g. Scīmus puellam **fuisse** fēlīcem.
We know (that) the girl was happy.

(*b*) **Sē** is used if (i) the **Subject** of the **Infinitive** is the **same** as that of the **Main Verb** and is **Third Person,** (ii) the **Object** of the **Infinitive** is the **same** as the **Subject** of the **Main Verb** and is **Third Person.**

e.g. Dīxit **sē** ventūrum esse. He *said* he *would come.*
Dīxit nōs **sibi** persuāsisse. He *said we had persuaded* him.

Eum, eam, etc. are used when the **Subject** or **Object** is different.

e.g. Dīximus { **eam** interfectam esse.
eam eōs interfectūram esse.

We said that { *she had been killed.*
she would kill them.

(*c*) **Spērō,** *I hope,* **promittō,** *I promise,* **iūrō,** *I swear,* **minor,** *I threaten* are followed by an **Accusative** and **Future Infinitive.**

e.g. Spērābant **sē ventūrōs esse.** *They hoped to come.*
Prōmīsimus **nōs mānsūrōs esse.** *We promised to stay.*

(*d*) **Negō,** *I deny, say . . . not,* is used; never dico . . . non.

e.g. **Negāvit** sē ventūrum esse. *He said he would not come.*

Thus, **negāre quemquam,** *to say that . . . no one*
negāre quidquam, *to say that . . . nothing*
negāre umquam, *to say that . . . never*
negāre usquam, *to say that . . . nowhere*

105. *Rule of Sequence*

In many Latin constructions in which the **Subjunctive** is used, the **Rule of Sequence** is observed. This is a simple method of dividing English tenses into two groups. This rule applies to the **Main Verb** and the **Tense** of the **Subjunctive** to be used will depend on the **Sequence** of the **Main Verb.**

Present
Future
Perfect with have } **Primary Tenses of the Indicative.**
Imperative
Future Perfect

Imperfect
Perfect without have } **Historic (Secondary) Tenses of the Indicative.**
Pluperfect

106. *Indirect Command*

(*a*) Venī, *Come,* is a Direct Command

Mē rogāvit **ut venīrem,** *He asked me to come,* is an **Indirect**

Command. Thus in Latin **ut** is used, negative **nē** with a **Present** or **Imperfect Subjunctive** according to **Sequence** to express an **Indirect Command.** This construction occurs after such verbs as **moneō,** *I warn*, **rogō,** *I ask*, **imperō,** *I order*, etc.

e.g. Mihi imperāvit **ut festīnārem.** *He ordered me to hurry.*
Monēbuntur **nē canant.** *They will be advised not to sing.*

N.B. In English an **Indirect Command** is most often shown by a **plain Infinitive.**

(*b*) Only two Latin Verbs take the English construction, **iubeō,** *I order*, and **vetō,** *I order . . . not, forbid.*

e.g. Iussī eōs **sequī.** *I* {*ordered* / *told*} *them to follow.*

Vetuī eōs **sequī.** *I* {*ordered* / *told*} *them not to follow.*

N.B. Iubeō and **vetō** may be translated by **tell** in the sense of **order.**

(*c*) **Sē** is used if the **Object** of the **Subordinate Verb** is the same as the **Subject** of the **Main Verb** and is **Third Person.**

e.g. Nōs hortātus est ut **sibi** librum ostenderēmus.
He *urged us to show* him *the book.*

107. *Indirect Question*

(*a*) Quid dīcis? *What are you saying?* is a Direct Question. Nesciō **quid dīcās?** *I do not know what you are saying*, is an **Indirect Question.** Thus in Latin the **Verb** of the **Indirect Question** goes into the **Subjunctive** and the clause is introduced by such words as **quis, quid, quandō, quārē, quot** etc. **Six Subjunctives** may be used.

Main Verb Primary {
Present Subjunctive
Perfect Subjunctive
-ūrus sim (*will*)
}

Main Verb Historic {
Imperfect Subjunctive
Pluperfect Subjunctive
-ūrus essem (*would*)
}

Golden Rule
The Verb in the **Principal Clause** decides the **Sequence,** the verb in the **Subordinate Clause** decides the **Tense** of the **Subjunctive** to be used.

e.g. Nesciō **quandō** { **redeās.** / **redieris.** / **reditūrus sīs.** }

I do not know when you { *are returning.* / *returned.* / *will return.* }

Nesciēbam **quid** { **facerēs.** / **fēcissēs.** / **factūrus essēs.** }

I did not know what you { *were doing.* / *had done.* / *would do.* }

(*b*) **Num,** *if, whether*

Utrum . . . an(necne), { *if . . .* / *whether* } *or* (*not*) are also used to introduce **Indirect Questions.**

e.g. Certior nōn factus est **utrum** pervēnissēs **necne.**

He was not told { *if* / *whether* } *you had arrived or not.*

(*c*) **Sē** is used as in Indirect Command to refer to the **Subject** of the **Main Verb.**

e.g. Rogāvit num **sē** adiūtūrī essēmus.
He *asked if we would help* him.

108. *Purpose Clauses*
(*a*) In Latin **ut,** negative **nē,** is used with the **Present** or **Imperfect Subjunctive** according to **Sequence** to express the **Purpose** of an action.

e.g. Venit **ut** rēgīnam **videat.**

He is coming { *in order that he may see the queen.* / *in order to see the queen.* / *to see the queen.* }

Domī manēbant **nē vidērentur.**

They stayed at home { *in order that they might not be seen.* / *in order not to be seen.* }

(*b*) **Quō** is used instead of **ut** if the **Purpose Clause** contains a **Comparative Adjective** or **Adverb.**

e.g. Collem ascendērunt **quō facilius** vallem vidērent.
They climbed the hill to see the valley more easily.

(*c*) **Quī – quae – quod** is often used instead of **ut** when there is an **Antecedent** in the **Accusative Case.**

e.g. **Gladium** mihi dedit **quō** ūterer.
He gave me a sword to use.
Lintrem inveniam in **quā** flūmen trānseam.
I shall find a boat in which to cross the river.

(*d*) **Sē** is used to refer to the **Subject** of the **Main Verb** if **Third Person.**

e.g. Hanc ōrātiōnem habuit nē **sē** culpārēmus.
He *made this speech that we might not blame* him.

For other ways of expressing Purpose, vid. secs. 95, 96, 128.

109. *Result Clauses*

(*a*) In Latin **ut,** negative **ut nōn,** with the **Subjunctive** is used to express the **Result** of an action.

e.g. Tam sapienter dīcit **ut** omnibus **persuādeat.**
He speaks so wisely that he persuades everybody.
Tantum saxum erat **ut nēmō** id tollere **posset.**
The stone was so big that no one could lift it.
Hostēs tot erant **ut fūgerimus.**
The enemy were so numerous that we fled.

N.B. In a Result Clause the **Perfect Subjunctive** may be used to stress the fact that the result actually did occur, i.e. **a once and for all action.**

(*b*) **Tam,** *so*, is used with **Adjectives** or **Adverbs.**
Ita, adeō, *so*, are used with **Verbs.**

e.g. **Adeō** īrāscēbatur ut omnēs eum timerēmus.
He was so angry that we all feared him.

N.B. Sē is **not** used to refer to Subject of Main Verb if Third Person.

(*c*) Note the following table.

	PURPOSE	RESULT
so that not	**nē**	**ut nōn**
so that no one	**nē quis**	**ut nēmō**
so that nothing	**nē quid**	**ut nihil**
so that none	**nē** { **ūllus** / **quī** }	**ut nūllus**
so that never	**nē umquam**	**ut numquam**
so that nowhere	**nē usquam**	**ut nusquam**

110. *Conditional Clauses*

(*a*) In Latin the **Indicative** is used in the **if** clause when the **Principal Clause** makes a **plain statement of fact.**

e.g. Sī hōc **facis,** stultus es.
If you do this, you are foolish.
Sī hōc **fēcistī,** stultus erās.
If you did this, you were foolish.
Sī hōc **fēceris,** poenās dabis.
If you do this, you will be punished.

N.B. (i) Latin logically uses the **Future Perfect** in the last example as it argues that you cannot be punished until **you will have done this.**

(ii) Latin uses the **Future** when the **if** verb is going on at the **same time** as the **Main Verb.**

e.g. Sī Rōmae **eris,** tē vīsam.
If you are in Rome, I shall visit you.

These are often called **Open Conditions.**

(*b*) In Latin the **Subjunctive** is used in **both** clauses when the **Principal Clause** merely states a **possibility,** i.e. that something **would, should** or **would have** happened.

e.g. Sī hōc **faciās,** poenās **dēs.**
If you were to do this, you would be punished.
Sī hōc **facerēs,** fēlīx **essēs.**
If you were doing this, you would be happy.
Sī hōc **fēcissēs,** poenās **dedissēs.**
If you had done this, you would have been punished.

Thus in table form

2 × Present Subjunctive = *were to* . . . { *would* / *should* }

2 × Imperfect Subjunctive = *were* . . . { *would* / *should* }

2 × Pluperfect Subjunctive = *had* . . . { *would* / *should* } *have*

Such Conditions referring to the **Present** or **Past** are often called **Unfulfilled Conditions.**

(*c*) **Sī** = *if*
Nisi = *unless*

Sī . . . non = *if . . . not* (where only **one** word is negatived not the whole clause).

e.g. Sī librum, **nōn** tabulam ēmerit, gaudēbō.
If he buys a book not a picture, I shall be glad.

Si quis = *if anyone.*

111. *Verbs of Fearing*

In Latin Verbs of Fearing, e.g. **timeō, vereor** are followed by **nē** if **Positive, nē nōn** or **ut** if **Negative** with the **Present** or **Perfect Subjunctive** after a **Primary Main Verb,** the **Imperfect** or **Pluperfect** after an **Historic Main Verb.**

e.g. Timeō **nē redeat.**

I am afraid that he { *is returning.* / *may return.* / *will return.* }

Verēbar **ut redīret.**

I feared that he { *was not returning.* / *might not return.* / *would not return.* }

Timēmus **nē nōn redierit.**

We fear that he has not returned.

N.B. (i) Ut can be used for **nē nōn** after **vereor** if **positive, timeō** always takes **nē nōn.**

(ii) Verbs of Fearing can be followed by an **Infinitive.**

e.g. Timēbat **loquī.**

He was afraid to speak.

(iii) Sē is used to refer to **Subject** of **Main Verb** if **Third Person.**

e.g. Mīles vulnerātus verēbātur ut **sē** vīdissēmus.

The wounded soldier *feared we had not seen* him.

112. *Verbs of Doubting*

Dubitō, *I doubt* and **dubius,** *doubtful* if **Negative** are followed by **quīn** with **Six Subjunctives.**

e.g. Nōn dubitāmus **quīn** novae cōpiae { **perveniant.** / **pervēnerint.** / **perventūrae sint.** }

We { *do not doubt* / *have no doubt* } *that reinforcements* { *are arriving.* / *have arrived.* / *will arrive.* }

Haud dubium erat **quīn** nāvis { **venīret.** / **vēnisset.** / **ventūra esset.** }

There was no doubt that the ship { *was coming.* / *had come.* / *would come.* }

N.B. (i) { **Quis** / **Vix quisquam** } dubitat, { *Who* / *scarcely anyone* } doubts, count as **Negative** and are therefore followed by **quīn** with the **Subjunctive.**

(ii) Sē is used to refer to **Subject** of **Main Verb** if **Third Person.**

e.g. Captīvus nōn dubitābat quīn **sē** ēreptūrī essēmus.
The captive *had no doubt that we would save* him.

(iii) Dubitō if **Negative** and followed by an **Infinitive** means *I hesitate.*

e.g. Puer **nōn** dubitāvit pilam **iacere.**
The boy did not hesitate to throw the ball.

113. *Simple Causal Clauses*

(*a*) **Quod, quia,** *because,* **quoniam,** *since, as,* are followed by the **Indicative.**

e.g. Puella lacrimābat {**quod** / **quia**} canem **amīserat.**
The girl was crying because she had lost her dog.
Quoniam vēnistī, mē adiuvāre dēbēs.
Since you have come, you ought to help me.

(*b*) **Cum,** *since, as,* is followed by the **Subjunctive.**

e.g. **Cum** ad flūmen **advēnisset,** pontem trānsīre cōnstituit.
Since he had reached the river, he decided to cross the bridge.

114. *Simple Concessive Clauses*

(*a*) **Quamquam,** *although,* is followed by the **Indicative.**

e.g. **Quamquam** hostēs superiōrēs numerō **erant,** eōs adortī sumus.
Although the enemy were superior in numbers, we attacked them.

(*b*) **Cum,** *although,* is followed by the **Subjunctive.**

e.g. **Cum** īnferiōrēs numerō **essēmus,** in hostēs impetum fēcimus.
Although we were inferior in numbers, we attacked the enemy.

115. *Temporal Clauses*

Dum

(*a*) **Dum,** *while, as long as,* is always followed by the **Indicative.** A **Present Indicative** is used if the **dum** Verb lasts **longer** than the Main Verb. If the **dum Verb,** lasts the **same** length of time as the **Main Verb,** it goes into the **same** tense as the **Main Verb.**

e.g. **Dum** Rōmae **sum,** Cicerōnem vīdī.
While I was in Rome, I saw Cicero.
Dum Rōmae **eram,** apud Cicerōnem **manēbam.**
While I was in Rome, I stayed with Cicero.
Dum Rōmae **eris,** apud Cicerōnem **manēbis.**
As long as you are in Rome, you will stay with Cicero.

(*b*) **Dum,** *until,* takes the **Indicative** if nothing but **Pure Time** is indicated, i.e. that the action simply took place.

e.g. **Dum** nūntius **rediit,** pavor in urbe erat.
Until the messenger returned, there was panic in the city.

Dōnec, quoad, *until,* are often found in this type of clause.

(*c*) **Dum,** *until,* takes the **Subjunctive, Present** or **Imperfect** when **Purpose** or **Design** is implied, frequently after **Verbs** of **waiting.**

e.g. **Sedē** ibī **dum redeam.**
Sit there until I return.
Exspectābant dum novae cōpiae in cōnspectum **venīrent.**
They waited { *until the reinforcements should come into view.* / *for the reinforcements to come into view.* }

116. *Cum*

(*a*) **Cum,** *when,* takes the **Indicative** if the **Main Verb** is **Primary.**

e.g. **Cum** tēcum **sum,** fēlīx sum.
When I am with you, I am happy.
Cum Rōmam **vēneris,** Cicerōnem vidēbis.
When you come (i.e. will have come) to Rome, you will see Cicero.
Cum Rōmae **eris,** lūdōs vidēbis.
When you are (i.e. will be) in Rome, you will see the games.

Note the accuracy of the Latin tenses.

(*b*) **Cum,** *when,* takes the **Subjunctive (Imperfect** or **Pluperfect)** if the **Main Verb** is **Historic.**

e.g. **Cum** ad flūmen **vēnissent,** ad alteram rīpam nāvērunt.
When they came to the river, they swam to the other bank.
Cum per silvam **ambulāret,** lupum vīdit.
When he was walking through the wood, he saw a wolf.

(*c*) **Cum,** *whenever,* takes the **Perfect Indicative** if the **Main Verb** is **Primary,** the **Pluperfect Indicative** if the **Main Verb** is **Historic.**

e.g. **Cum** mē **vīdit,** rīdet.
Whenever he sees me, he smiles.
Cum mē **vīderat,** rīdēbat.
Whenever he saw me, he {smiled. / would smile.}

117. *Ubī, Postquam, Simulac*

(*a*) **Ubī,** *when,* **postquam,** *after,* **simulac,** *as soon as,* take a **Perfect Indicative** if the **Main Verb** is **Historic.**

e.g. {**Ubī** / **Postquam** / **Simulac**} **cōnfessus est,** capitis damnātus est.
{*When* / *After* / *As soon as*} *he (had) confessed, he was condemned to death.*

(*b*) Only **postquam** can take a **Pluperfect Indicative** if a **definite** period of time is mentioned.

e.g. **Decem post diēbus quam redierat,** mortem obiit.
Ten days after he had returned, he died.

N.B. Ubī, simulac may be followed by a **Future** a **Future Perfect** like **cum.**

e.g. {**Ubī** / **Simulac**} **pervēneris,** rēgem vidēbis.
{*When* / *As soon as*} *you arrive, you will see the king.*

118. *Antequam, Priusquam*

(*a*) **Antequam, priusquam,** *before,* take the **Indicative** if nothing but **Pure Time** is indicated, i.e. that the action simply took place.

e.g. Mīlitem **prius** interfēcit **quam pervēnī.**
He killed the soldier before I arrived.
Antequam cubitum **eō,** fenestram aperiam.
Before I go to bed, I shall open the window.
Nōn **prius** discēdam **quam** mihi vēra **dīxeris.**
I shall not leave {before / until} you tell me the truth.

N.B. Latin tenses used with **priusquam** and **antequam** are the **same** as those used in English except if the **Main Verb** is **Negative Future** when a **Future Perfect** is used in the 'before' clause.

(*b*) **Antequam, priusquam** take a **Present** or **Imperfect Subjunctive** when **Purpose** or **Design** is implied, i.e. that the action of the Main Verb takes place before that of the Subordinate Verb **can** happen.

e.g. **Priusquam** portās **clauderent,** armātī in oppidum ruērunt.
Before they could *close the gates, armed men rushed into the town.*
Puer ex agrō **prius** cucurrit **quam** agricola **sē prohibēret.**
The boy ran from the field before the farmer could *stop him.*

N.B. Sē is used to refer to the **Subject** of the **Main Verb** as **Purpose** is implied.

119. *Comparative Clauses*

(*a*) In Latin the **Indicative** is used to indicate a **Real Comparison,** i.e. English **'as'.**

e.g. Mea māter **eadem** est {**ac** / **quae**} abhinc annōs vīgintī **erat.**
My mother is the same as she was twenty years ago.
Tot aquilās nōn vīdimus **quot exspectābāmus.**
We did not see as many eagles as we expected.
Tam fortis est **quam** leō.
He is as brave as a lion.

The following list contains the common phrases used in Latin to introduce a **Real Comparison.**

tam . . . quam	*as . . . as*
tantus . . . quantus	*as great . . . as*
tot . . . quot	*as many . . . as*
tālis . . . quālis	*such a kind . . . as*
totiēs . . . quotiēs	*so often . . . as*
īdem . . . {ac / quī}	*the same . . . as*
sīcut	*just as*
haud {aliter / secus} ac	*not otherwise than*
perinde ac	*exactly as*

(*b*) In Latin the **Subjunctive** is used to indicate an **Imaginary Comparison,** i.e. English **'as if'.**

e.g. Sē gerit **velutsī** īnsānus **esset.**
He behaves as if he were mad.
Sē gessit **velutsī** imāginem **vīdisset.**
He behaved as if he had seen a ghost.

N.B. Velutsī observes **Conditional** rules, **quasi** observes **Sequence** rules.

e.g. Sē gerit **quasi** īnsānus **sit.**

120. *Sub-Oblique Clauses, i.e. Subordinate Clauses in Reported Speech.*
In Latin if an **Adjective** or **Adverbial Clause** is **Subordinate** to an **Indirect Statement, Command** or **Question,** i.e. is **part** of the **direct words** its **Verb** goes into the **Subjunctive.**

e.g. DIRECT
Cum mīles redierit, eum vidēbimus.
When the soldier returns, we shall see him.

INDIRECT
Dīximus nōs, cum mīles **rediisset,** eum vīsūrōs esse.
We said that when the soldier returned we would see him.

DIRECT

Cur librum quem tibi dedī, amīsistī?
Why have you lost the book I gave you?

INDIRECT

Scīre volō cur librum quem tibi **dederim,** amīseris.
I want to know why you have lost the book I gave you.

DIRECT

Recitā carmen quod didicistī.
Recite the poem you have learned.

INDIRECT

Magister mē iussit carmen quod **didicissem** recitāre.
The teacher told me to recite the poem I had learned.

N.B. The **Tense** of the Subjunctive to be used is found by going back to the **Direct Words** and then applying the following table.

DIRECT TENSE	MAIN VERB PRIMARY	MAIN VERB HISTORIC
Present	**Present Subjunctive**	**Imperfect Subjunctive**
Imperfect	**Imperfect Subjunctive**	**Imperfect Subjunctive**
Perfect	**Perfect Subjunctive**	**Pluperfect Subjunctive**
Pluperfect	**Pluperfect Subjunctive**	**Pluperfect Subjunctive**
Future	**Present Subjunctive**	**Imperfect Subjunctive**
Future Perfect	**Perfect Subjunctive**	**Pluperfect Subjunctive**

Additional Syntax

XXI. NOUNS

121. *Accusative*

(*a*) The **Accusative** is found, particularly in poetry, after an **Adjective** to define more exactly the meaning of the **Adjective.**

e.g. Flāva **comās.** *Fair haired.* (lit. *fair as to the hair.*)
Fēminae nūdae **bracchia** et **lacertōs.**
Women with their lower and upper arms bare.
(lit. *women bare as to their lower and upper arms.*)

(*b*) The **Accusative** is found, particularly in poetry, after a **Perfect Participle Passive** to denote the **part of the body** affected.

e.g. **Femur** trāgulā ictus.
Wounded in the thigh by a javelin.
(lit. *wounded as to the thigh. . . .*)
Subtūsa **genās.** *With her cheeks bruised.*
(lit. *bruised as to her cheeks.*)

(*c*) The **Accusative** is found, mostly in poetry, after a **Passive Verb** which is really **Reflexive** in meaning, i.e. the **Subject** is doing something to or for **himself.**

e.g. **Lōrīcam** induitur. *He dons his breastplate.*
Laevō suspēnsī **loculōs tabulāsque** lacertō.
Slinging their schoolbags and writing pads over their left arms.
Conversī **lūmina.** *Turning their eyes.*

122. *Genitive*

(*a*) The **Genitive** may follow another Noun to denote that the **Genitive** is the **Subject** of the activity.

e.g. Timor **populī.** *The fear of the people.* (i.e. *the people fear.*)
Veterēs **Helvētiōrum** iniūriae.
The ancient wrongs of the Helvetii.
(i.e. *The Helvetii committed ancient wrongs.*)

(*b*) The **Genitive** may follow another Noun to denote that the **Genitive** is the **Object** of the activity.

e.g. Timor **populī.** *The fear of the people.* (i.e. *we fear the people.*)
Veterēs Helvētiōrum iniūriae **populī Rōmānī.**
The ancient wrongs of the Helvetii on the Roman people.
(i.e. *The Helvetii wronged the Roman people.*)

(*c*) The **Genitive** is used with the verb **to be** to mean, *duty of, mark of, characteristic of.*

e.g. **Mīlitis** est pugnāre. *It is the duty of a soldier to fight.*
Discipulōrum est tempus terere.
It is characteristic of pupils to waste time.

123. *Dative*

(*a*) The **Dative** is sometimes used after a **Perfect Passive** to denote the **Agent.**

e.g. Rēs tōta **mihi** prōvīsa est.
The whole business has been arranged by me.

(For Dative of Agent after Gerundive, vid. sec. 96b.)

(*b*) The **Dative** is used to indicate the **purpose aimed at** (vid. sec. 73c).

e.g. **Receptuī** cecinit. *He sounded the retreat.*
Comitia **cēnsōribus creāndīs** habuit.
He held a meeting for electing censors.

(*c*) The **Dative** is used in poetry to indicate **motion towards.**

e.g. It clamor **caelō.** *The shouting reaches the heavens.*

(*d*) The **Dative** of a **Pronoun** can be used to indicate a person **interested** in the action.

e.g. Quid **mihi** Celsus agit? *How, please, is Celsus doing?*

124. *Ablative*

(*a*) The **Ablative** is used with a **Comparative** to indicate how much something or somebody is **different** from something or somebody else.

e.g. Hibernia **dīmidiō** minor est quam Britannia.
Ireland is half as small as Britain.

Paulō		*little*	
Aliquantō	altior est. *He is*	*considerably*	*taller.*
Multō		*much*	

(*b*) The **Ablative** is used to indicate **Separation.**

e.g. **Dēfēnsōribus** castra nūdāvit.
He stripped the camp of defenders.
Hostēs **commeātū** intercludere cōnstituit.
He decided to cut the enemy off from their supplies.

(*c*) The **Ablative** is used to define more closely in what **Respect** the statement is made.

e.g. Quattuor mīlia **numerō.** *Four thousand in number.*
Ferōx **ingeniō.** *Fierce in character.*
Captus **alterō oculō.** *Blind in one eye.*

XXII. RELATIVE CLAUSES

125. (*a*) A **Superlative** or **Numeral Adjective** is attracted from the **Antecedent** into the **Relative Clause.**

e.g. Equōs quōs **optimōs** habeō, vendam.
I shall sell the best horses I have.
Barbarō quem **prīmum** vīdit pepercit.
He spared the first native he saw.

(*b*) The **Antecedent** is often repeated in the **Relative Clause.**

e.g. Silvam prope castra sitam animadvertit quā in **silvā** equitēs cēlāvit.
He spotted a wood near the camp in which he hid his cavalry.

XXIII. VERBS

126. *Epistolary Imperfect*

The **Imperfect** is often used in **letters** to refer to the time of writing, i.e. the writer puts himself in the place of the recipient and uses the **Imperfect** for the Present.

e.g. Nihil **habēbam** quod plūs scrīberem.
I have nothing more to write.

127. *Indicative*

The following idiomatic use of the **Indicative** should be noted.

Facile **est.** *It would be easy.*
Facile {**erat** / **fuit**}. *It would have been easy.*

128. *First Supine*

The **First Supine** is used after **Verbs of Motion** to express **Purpose.**

e.g. **Cubitum** īvērunt. *They went to bed.*
Tertiam cohortem **frūmentātum** mīsit.
He sent the third cohort to forage.

129. *Subjunctive*

(*a*) In Latin the **Subjunctive** is used when a **Question** is asked implying **bewilderment** or **indecision.** This is called a **Deliberative Question.**

e.g. Quid **dīcam**? *What am I to say?*
Quid **dīcerem**? *What was I to say?*
Quō **īrent**? *Where were they to go?*

(*b*) In Latin the **Subjunctive** is used to express a **Possibility,** really a **Condition** with the **if** clause omitted. This is called a **Potential Subjunctive.**

Velim venīre. *I should like to come.*
Vellem venīre. *I should have liked to come.*
Velim veniās. *I should like you to come.*
Vellem vēnissēs. *I should have liked you to come.*

N.B. The subjunctives **veniās** and **vēnisses** are best taken as Wishes for the Future and Past respectively, i.e. *I should like you to come* = *O that you may come.*

XXIV. PLACE

130. (*a*) In Latin it is possible to have a **Double Accusative** of **Motion.**

e.g. **In castra ad ducem** vēnit.
He came to the general in the camp.

(*b*) In Latin **ad** is found with the **Name** of a **Town** to mean, *in the neighbourhood of*, or *in the direction of.*

e.g. Proelium **ad Cannās** factum.
The battle fought at Cannae.
Ad Ilerdam proficīscitur.
He set out in the direction of Ilerda.

(*c*) The Verb **absum** takes **a**(**b**) even with the **Names** of **Towns** as no motion is implied.

e.g. Decem mīlia passuum **ā Vēiīs** aberant.
They were ten miles distant from Veii.

(*d*) **Domus** may take the Preposition **in** when it means *house.*

e.g. **In** domum iniit. *He entered the house.*

XXV. SUBORDINATE CONSTRUCTIONS

131. *Indirect Statement*

(*a*) As some Latin Verbs do not have a **Supine,** and therefore cannot form the **Future Infinitive, fore ut** with a **Present** or **Imperfect Subjunctive** is used as follows.

e.g. Puer dīxit **fore ut** hōs versūs **disceret.**
The boy said he would learn these verses.
Prō certō habēmus **fore ut** nostrī hostibus **resistant.**
We are sure our men will resist the enemy.

(*b*) In Indirect Statement the **Future Infinitive Passive** is somewhat rare, **fore ut** is usually preferred.

e.g. Rēx certior factus est **fore ut** fēminae **servārentur.**
The king was informed that the women would be saved.

(*c*) **Simulō,** *pretend* and **dissimulō,** *pretend . . . not,* are followed by an **Accusative** and **Infinitive.**

e.g. Simulābāmus **nōs aegrōs esse.**
We pretended to be ill.
Puer dissimulābat **sē** librum **amīsisse.**
The boy pretended he had not lost the book.

(*d*) **Vidētur,** *it seems,* **dīcitur,** *it is said,* **putātur,** *it is thought,* **nūntiātur,** *it is announced,* are used **Personally** in the **Present, Future** and **Imperfect Tenses.**

e.g. **Vidēris** esse dīves.
It seems that you are rich.
Putābāmur interfectī esse.
It was thought that we had been killed.

N.B. In the **Perfect Tenses** these Verbs are used **Impersonally** as in English.

e.g. **Nūntiātum est** hostēs appropinquāre.
It was announced that the enemy were approaching.

(*e*) Verbs of **Emotion,** e.g. **gaudeō,** *be glad,* **doleō,** *be sorry,* **mīror,** *be surprised that,* can be followed by (i) **Indirect Statement** (ii) **Quod** with the **Indicative.**

e.g. Dolēbant { **tē** nōn **rediisse.**
{ **quod** nōn **redierās.**
They were sorry you had not returned.

132. *Nēve, Neu*

If a **Positive Purpose Clause** or **Indirect Command** is followed by a **Negative One, nēve (neu)** introduces the **second** one.

e.g. Rōmam vēnit ut studeat **nēve** tempus terat.
He has come to Rome to study and not to waste time.
Cōnsul suōs hortātus est ut resisterent **neu** sē traderent.
The consul encouraged his men to resist and not to surrender.

133. *Quī Generic*

In Latin **quī – quae – quod** is often used with the **Subjunctive** to mean, *the sort of person to* or *the kind of person to.*

e.g. Is est **quī** urbem **servet.**
He is the man to save the city.
(lit. *he is the sort of person who may save the city.*)
Erant **quī** cōnsulem **culpārent.**
There were some who blamed the consul.
(lit. *there were those of the kind who might blame the consul.*)

Other such phrases are:

dīgnus est quī	*he deserves to*
ea est quae	*she is the woman to*
aptus est quī	*he is fit to*
nihil habeō quod	*I have nothing to*

134. *Comparison*

(*a*) In Latin the **Comparative** is used with **quam quī (ut)** and the **Subjunctive** to mean *too . . . to.*

e.g. Puer erat **stultior quam** {**quī** / **ut**} hunc librum **intellegeret.**
The boy was too stupid to understand this book.
Gladius est **gravior quam** {**quem** / **ut**} **tollam.**
The sword is too heavy for me to raise.

(*b*) In Latin **quō** and the **Comparative** followed by **eō** and the **Comparative** means *the more . . . the more.*

e.g. **Quō citius, eō melius.** *The sooner, the better.*
Quō plūs vīnī **quis** bibit, **eō magis** id amat.
The more wine a man drinks, the more he likes it.

N.B. Quis after **quō** means *a man* or *anyone.*

135. *Conditional Clauses*

(*a*) In Latin **sīve(seu) . . . sīve(seu)** introduce a **Double Condition.**

e.g. **Sīve** ille damnātus esset **sīve** absolūtus esset, nēmō eī crēdidisset.
Whether that man had been condemned or acquitted no one would have believed him.

Sīve Pompēiīs mānseris, **sīve nōn** mānseris, Rōmam redībimus.
Whether you stay in Pompeii or not, we shall return to Rome.

(*b*) In an **Unfulfilled Condition** it is possible to have the **sī** clause referring to **Past Time** and the **Principal Clause** to **Present Time.**

e.g. Sī dīligentius **labōrāvissēmus,** hodiē dīvitēs **essēmus.**
If we had worked harder, we would be rich today.

(*c*) In an **Unfulfilled Condition,** the **Indicative** is used in the **Principle Clause** with the following verbs, **possum, dēbeō,** and with the **Gerundive** expressing **Obligation.**

e.g. Sī rediissent, servārī **potuērunt.**
If they had returned, they could have been saved.
Sī hōc fēcisset, damnandus **fuit.**
If he had done this, he would have had to be condemned.

136. *Alleged Reason and Qui Causal*

(*a*) In Latin **quod** is used with the **Subjunctive** to indicate that the reason is **alleged** or **supposed** and not a **definite** fact, shown in English by such phrases as, *on the grounds that, for having, because as they said.*

e.g. In vincula cōniectus est **quod** patriam **prōdidisset.**

He was thrown into prison { *on the grounds that he had betrayed his native land.* / *for having betrayed his native land.* / *because, as they said, he had betrayed his native land.* }

N.B. Nōn quod with the **Subjunctive . . . sed quia** with the **Indicative** means *not because* (alleged reason) . . . *but because* (true reason).

e.g. Tē culpō **nōn quod** stultus **sīs, sed quia** īgnāvus **es.**
I blame you not because you are foolish, but because you are lazy.

N.B. In an **Alleged Reason sē** is used to refer to the **Subject** of the **Main Verb** if **Third Person.**

e.g. Is eques mē ōderat quod **sibi** nocuissem.
That knight *hated me because, as he maintained, I had injured* him.

(*b*) In Latin **quī** can be used with the **Subjunctive** to express **Cause.**

e.g. Mihi īrāscēbātur **quī** ē castrīs **discessissem.**
He was angry with me for leaving the camp.

137. *Concessive Clauses*

(*a*) In Latin **licet, ut, nē,** are used with the **Subjunctive** to concede a fact for the sake of the argument, shown in English by such phrases as, **granted that, suppose that.**

e.g. {**Licet** / **Ut**} **sit** improbus; ūtilis tamen reīpūblicae est.
Granted that he is wicked; yet he is useful to the state.
Nē sit summum malum dolor, malum certē est.
Suppose that pain is not the worst evil, yet surely it is still an evil.

(*b*) In Latin **quamvīs** with the **Subjunctive** can mean (1) *although* (2) *however (much).*

e.g. **Quamvīs** cōnsul exercituī **praesit,** hostēs nōn vincēs.
Although the consul is in command of the army, you will not defeat the enemy.
Quamvīs dīves **sīs,** tē cōnsulem nōn creābunt.
However rich you {may be / are}, they will not elect you consul.

(*c*) In Latin **etsī, etiamsī,** *although, even if,* are used under **Conditional** rules.

e.g. {**Etsī** / **Etiamsī**} vēra **dīxisset,** iūdex eī nōn **pepercisset.**
{Even if / Although} he had told the truth, the judge would not have spared him.

(*d*) In Latin **quī** with the **Subjunctive** is occasionally used to introduce a **Concessive Clause. Tamen** is often present in the Principal Clause.

e.g. Ego **quī** idem **peccāverim,** tē **tamen** culpō.
Although I have committed the same sin myself, yet I blame you.

138. *Temporal Clauses*

(*a*) **Cum,** *when*, takes the **Indicative** if it expresses **Pure Time** only, and there is no suggestion of **Reason** or **Cause** which would require the Subjunctive. *When* means *at the time when*, and the Subjects of the two clauses are often different and contrasted.

e.g. **Cum** nōs Londīniī **erāmus,** tū Rōmae manēbās.
When we were in London, you were staying in Rome.

(*b*) **Cum,** *when*, takes the **Indicative** if it contains the **Principal** thought of the sentence, i.e. is equivalent to *and then.*

e.g. Ad focum sedēbāmus **cum** arāneam **animadvertimus.**
We were sitting at the hearth when we noticed the spider.

(*c*) In Latin **dummodo** is used with the **Subjunctive,** negative **nē,** to mean, *provided that, if only.*

e.g. Dīves fīēs **dummodo** lēgēs **nē violēs.**
You will become rich, provided you do not break the laws.

139. *Uses of Quin*

(*a*) In Latin **quīn** is used for **quī** (**Generic**) **non** after a **Negative, Virtually Negative** or **Interrogative Principal Clause.**

e.g. { **Nēmō** / **Quis** / **Vix quisquam** } est **quīn** linguam Latīnam **amet.**

{ *There is no one* / *Who is there* / *There is scarcely anyone* } *who does not like Latin.*

(*b*) In Latin such Verbs as **impediō,** *hinder*, **dēterreō,** *deter*, **recūsō,** *refuse*, if **Negative,** may be followed by **quīn** or **quōminus** with the **Subjunctive.**

e.g. Nōn recūsābat **quīn** sententiam **dīceret.**
He did not refuse to give his opinion.
Eum nōn dēterrēbimus **quōminus** Rōmā **discēdat.**
We shall not deter him from leaving Rome.

N.B. (i) These Verbs if **Positive** take **nē** or **quōminus.**

e.g. Eum dēterrēbimus {**nē** / **quōminus**} Rōmā **discēdat.**
We shall deter him from leaving Rome.

(ii) Quōminus is also found in the idiomatic phrase, **per mē stābat quōminus. . . .** *It was my fault that . . . not.*

e.g. **Per mē stābat quōminus** speculatōrēs **caperentur.**
It was my fault that the spies were not captured.

(*c*) In Latin **quīn** with the **Subjunctive** follows such phrases as:

facere nōn possum quīn	*I cannot help —ing*
haud multum abest quīn	*be within an ace of*
nihil praetermittō quīn	*I leave no stone unturned to*
fierī nōn potest quīn	*it must be that*

e.g. Facere nōn poterant **quīn rīdērent.**
They could not help laughing.
Haud multum āfuit **quīn** arx **caperētur.**
The citadel was within an ace of being captured.

Note that this idiom is always used **Impersonally,** as is the following one:

Fierī nōn potest **quīn mentiantur.**
They must be lying.

140. *Unfulfilled Past Conditions in Reported Speech*

(*a*) **In Indirect Statement**

The **sī** clause remains in the **Subjunctive,** the **Principal Clause** now becomes an **Indirect Statement** with its **Infinitive** in the form **-ūrum fuisse.**

e.g. DIRECT
Sī hōc scīvissēmus, vēnissēmus.
If we had known this, we would have come.

INDIRECT
Dīximus nōs, sī hōc scīvissēmus, **ventūrōs fuisse.**
We said that we would have come if we had known this.

(*b*) **In Indirect Question**

The **sī** clause remains in the **Subjunctive,** the **Principal Clause** now becomes an **Indirect Question** with its **Verb** in the form **-ūrus fuerim.**

e.g. DIRECT

Sī hōc scīvissēmus, vēnissēmus.

If we had known this, we would have come.

INDIRECT

Mīrābāmur num **ventūrī fuerimus,** sī hōc scīvissēmus.

We wondered whether we would have come if we had known this.

N.B. The Verb is also used in the form **-ūrus fuerim** after **Verbs of Doubting** and **Result Clauses.**

e.g. Haud dubium est quīn nōs **adiūtūrus fuerit** sī rogātus esset.

There is no doubt that he would have helped us if he had been asked.

Adeō īrāscēbātur ut nōs **ictūrus fuerit** nisi discessissēmus.

He was so angry that he would have struck us, had we not left.

141. PRINCIPAL PARTS OF COMMON IRREGULAR VERBS*

abdō -ĕre, **abdidī, abditum,** *put aside, hide*
abiciō -ĕre, **abiēcī, abiectum,** *throw away*
abigō -ĕre, **abēgī, abāctum,** *drive away*
abripiō -ĕre, **abripuī, abreptum,** *tear away*
accendō -ĕre, **accendī, accēnsum,** *set on fire*
accidō -ĕre, **accidī, ——,** *happen*
accīdō -ere, **accīdī, accīsum,** *cut*
accipiō -ĕre, **accēpī, acceptum,** receive
accumbō -ĕre, **accubuī, accubitum,** *lie down, lie at table*
accurrō -ĕre, **accurrī, accursum,** *run to*
addō -ĕre, **addidī, additum,** *add*
adimō -ĕre, **adēmī, ademptum,** *take away*
adipīscor -ī, **adeptus sum,** *obtain*
adiuvō -āre, **adiūvī, adiūtum,** *help*

* Common compounds of fero and eo are to be found on pages 38 and 40.

adorior -īrī, **adortus sum,** *attack*
afflīgō -ĕre, **afflīxī, afflīctum,** *damage, strike against*
aggredior -ī, **aggressus sum,** *attack*
agnōscō -ĕre, **agnōvī, agnitum,** *recognise*
agō -ĕre, **ēgī, āctum,** *do, drive*
alō -ĕre, **aluī, altum** *or* **alitum,** *nourish, rear*
amplector -ī, **amplexus sum,** *embrace*
aperiō -īre, **aperuī, apertum,** *open*
arcessō -ĕre, **arcessīvī, arcessītum,** *send for, fetch*
ārdeō -ēre, **ārsī, ārsum,** *be on fire*
arripiō -ĕre, **arripuī, arreptum,** *snatch*
ascendō -ĕre, **ascendī, ascēnsum,** *climb up*
aspiciō -ĕre, **aspexī, aspectum,** *look at*
attingō -ĕre, **attigī, attāctum,** *touch, reach*
augeō -ēre, **auxī, auctum,** *increase*
bibō -ĕre, **bibī, ——,** *drink*
cadō -ĕre, **cecidī, cāsum,** *fall*
caedō -ĕre, **cecīdī, caesum,** *cut*
canō -ĕre, **cecinī, cantum,** *sing*
capiō -ĕre, **cēpī, captum,** *take*
carpō -ĕre, **carpsī, carptum,** *pluck*
caveō -ēre, **cāvī, cautum,** *beware*
cēdō -ĕre, **cessī, cessum,** *go, yield*
cēnseō -ēre, **cēnsuī, cēnsum,** *think, propose*
cernō -ĕre, **crēvī, crētum,** *perceive*
cingō -ĕre, **cinxī, cinctum,** *surround*
circumdō -ăre, **circumdedī, circumdatum,** *put around, besiege*
circumstō -āre, **circumstetī, ——,** *stand around*
claudō -ĕre, **clausī, clausum,** *close, shut*
cognōscō -ĕre, **cognōvī, cognitum,** *get to know, learn*
cōgō -ĕre, **coēgī, coāctum,** *force, gather together*
colligō -ĕre, **collēgī, collēctum,** *collect*
colō -ĕre, **coluī, cultum,** *cultivate, inhabit, worship*
compellō -ĕre, **compulī, compulsum,** *force together*
comperiō -īre, **comperī, compertum,** *ascertain*
complector -ī, **complexus sum,** *embrace*

compleō -ēre, **complēvī, complētum,** *fill up*
comprimō -ĕre, **compressī, compressum,** *check, restrain*
concidō -ĕre, **concidī, ——,** *fall down*
concīdō -ĕre, **concīdī, concīsum,** *cut down*
condō -ĕre, **condidī, conditum,** *found, store, bury*
cōnficiō -ĕre, **cōnfēcī, cōnfectum,** *finish, complete*
cōnfiteor -ērī, **cōnfessus sum,** *confess*
coniciō -ĕre, **coniēcī, coniectum,** *throw together*
cōnsīdō -ĕre, **cōnsēdī, cōnsessum,** *sit down, take up position, encamp*
cōnsistō -ĕre, **cōnstitī, ——,** *halt*
cōnspiciō -ĕre, **cōnspexī, cōnspectum,** *catch sight of*
cōnstituō -ĕre, **cōnstituī, cōnstitūtum,** *decide, position*
cōnsulō -ĕre, **cōnsuluī, cōnsultum,** *consult*
contemnō -ĕre, **contempsī, contemptum,** *despise*
contendō -ĕre, **contendī, contentum,** *strive, hasten*
contingō -ĕre, **contigī, contāctum,** *touch*
coquō -ĕre, **coxī, coctum,** *cook*
corripiō -ĕre, **corripuī, correptum,** *seize*
crēdō -ĕre, **crēdidī, crēditum,** *believe*
crēscō -ĕre, **crēvī, crētum,** *grow*
cubō -āre, **cubuī, cubitum,** *lie down*
cupiō -ĕre, **cupīvī, cupītum,** *desire*
currō -ĕre, **cucurrī, cursum,** *run*
dēcernō -ĕre, **dēcrēvī, dēcrētum,** *decide, decree*
dēcipio -ĕre, **dēcēpī, dēceptum,** *deceive*
dēdō -ĕre, **dēdidī, dēditum,** *surrender*
dēfendō -ĕre, **dēfendī, dēfēnsum,** *defend*
dēficiō -ĕre, **dēfēcī, dēfectum,** *revolt, fail*
dēiciō -ĕre, **dēiēcī, dēiectum,** *throw down*
dēleō -ēre, **dēlēvī, dēlētum,** *destroy*
dēligō -ĕre, **dēlēgī, dēlectum,** *choose*
dēpellō -ĕre, **dēpulī, dēpulsum,** *drive away*
dēsiliō -īre, **dēsiluī, dēsultum,** *leap down*
dēsinō -ĕre, **dēsiī, dēsitum,** *cease*
dēsistō -ĕre, **dēstitī, ——,** *desist*
dēspiciō -ĕre, **dēspexī, dēspectum,** *despise, look down upon*

dētineō -ēre, **dētinuī, dētentum,** *keep back*
dīcō -ĕre, **dīxī, dictum,** *say*
dīligō -ĕre, **dīlēxī, dīlēctum,** *love*
dīmicō (1), *fight*
dirimō -ĕre, **dirēmī, dirēmptum,** *separate*
dīripiō -ĕre, **dīripuī, dīreptum,** *plunder*
discō -ĕre, **didicī, ——,** *learn*
dīvidō -ĕre, **dīvīsī, dīvīsum,** *divide*
dō -dăre, **dedī, datum,** *give*
doceō -ēre, **docuī, doctum,** *teach*
domō -āre, **domuī, domitum,** *tame*
dūcō -ĕre, **dūxī, ductum,** *lead*
edō -ĕre, **ēdī, ēsum,** *eat*
ēdō -ĕre, **ēdidī, ēditum,** *give out, cause*
efficiō -ĕre, **effēcī, effectum,** *contrive*
egeō -ēre, **eguī, ——,** *need*
ēgredior -ī, **ēgressus sum,** *go out*
ēligō -ĕre, **ēlēgī, ēlēctum,** *choose*
emō -ĕre, **ēmī, ēmptum,** *buy*
ēripiō -ĕre, **ēripuī, ēreptum,** *tear away, rescue*
ēvādō -ĕre, **ēvāsī, ēvāsum,** *go out, escape*
excipiō -ĕre, **excēpī, exceptum,** *catch up, snatch*
exclūdō -ĕre, **exclūsī, exclūsum,** *shut out*
expellō -ĕre, **expulī, expulsum,** *drive out*
experior -īrī, **expertus sum,** *test, risk*
exuō -ĕre, **exuī, exūtum,** *strip*
faciō -ĕre, **fēcī, factum,** *do, make*
fallō -ĕre, **fefellī, falsum,** *deceive*
for -fārī, **fātus sum,** *say, speak*
fateor -ērī, **fassus sum,** *confess*
faveō -ēre, **fāvī, fautum,** *favour*
feriō -īre, **percussī, ictum,** *strike*
fīdō -ĕre, **fīsus sum,** *trust*
fīgō -ĕre, **fīxī, fīxum,** *fix*
findō -ĕre, **fidī, fissum,** *split*
fingō -ĕre, **finxī, fictum,** *feign, invent*

flectō -ĕre, **flexī, flexum,** *bend*
fleō -ēre, **flēvī, flētum,** *weep*
flōreō -ēre, **flōruī, ——,** *flourish*
fluō -ĕre, **flūxī, ——,** *flow*
fodiō -ĕre, **fōdī, fossum,** *dig*
foveō -ēre, **fōvī, fōtum,** *cherish*
frangō -ĕre, **frēgī, frāctum,** *break*
fruor -ī, **frūctus** *or* **fruitus sum,** *enjoy*
fugiō -ĕre, **fūgī, fugitum,** *flee*
fulgeō -ēre, **fulsī, ——,** *gleam*
fundō -ĕre, **fūdī, fūsum,** *pour, rout*
fungor -ī, **fūnctus sum,** *perform*
furō -ĕre, **——,** *rage*
gaudeō -ēre, **gāvīsus sum,** *rejoice*
gemō -ĕre, **gemuī, gemitum,** *groan*
gerō -ĕre, **gessī, gestum,** *carry, manage*
gignō -ĕre, **genuī, genitum,** *beget, produce*
haereō -ēre, **haesī, haesum,** *stick*
haurio -īre, **hausī, haustum,** *drain*
hortor -ārī, **hortātus sum,** *encourage*
iaceō -ēre, **iacuī, ——,** *lie (down)*
iaciō -ĕre, **iēcī, iactum,** *throw*
īgnōscō -ĕre, **īgnōvī, īgnōtum,** *pardon*
immineō -ēre, **——, ——,** *overhang, threaten*
impellō -ĕre, **impulī, impulsum,** *drive on*
impendeō -ēre, **——, ——,** *overhang, threaten*
incendō -ĕre, **incendī, incēnsum,** *burn*
incidō -ĕre, **incidī, incāsum,** *fall into*
incīdō -ĕre, **incīdī, incīsum,** *cut into*
incipiō -ĕre, **coepī, coeptum,** *begin*
inclūdō -ĕre, **inclūsī, inclūsum,** *shut in*
incumbō -ĕre, **incubuī, incubitum,** *lie on*
indulgeō -ēre, **indulsī, indultum,** *gratify*
induō -ĕre, **induī, indūtum,** *put on*
īnflīgō -ĕre, **īnflīxī, īnflīctum,** *strike against*
ingredior -ī, **ingressus sum,** *enter*

iniciō -ĕre, **iniēcī, iniectum,** *throw into*

intellegō -ĕre, **intellēxī, intellēctum,** *understand*

interclūdō -ĕre, **interclūsī, interclūsum,** *cut off*

interficiō -ĕre, **interfēcī, interfectum,** *kill*

īrāscor -ī, **īrātus sum,** *be angry*

iubeō -ēre, **iussī, iussum,** *order*

iungō -ĕre, **iūnxī, iūnctum,** *join*

iuvō -āre, **iūvī, iūtum,** *help*

lābor -ī, **lāpsus sum,** *slip, glide*

lacessō -ĕre, **lacessīvī, lacessītum,** *provoke*

laedō -ĕre, **laesī, laesum,** *harm*

lateō -ēre, **latuī, ——,** *lie hidden*

lavō -āre, **lāvī,** { **lautum** / **lavātum** / **lōtum** }, *wash*

legō -ĕre, **lēgī, lēctum,** *read, choose*

licet -ēre, **licuit, ——,** *it is allowed*

linquō -ĕre, **līquī, ——,** *leave, abandon*

loquor -ī, **locūtus sum,** *speak*

lūdō -ĕre, **lūsī, lūsum,** *play*

lūgeō -ēre, **lūxī, ——,** *mourn*

mālō -mālle, **māluī, ——,** *prefer*

maneō -ēre, **mānsī, mānsum,** *stay*

meminī, meminisse, ——, *remember*

mentior -īrī, **mentītus sum,** *tell a lie*

mergō -ĕre, **mersī, mersum,** *sink*

mētior -īrī, **mēnsus sum,** *measure*

metuō -ĕre, **metuī, ——,** *fear*

minuō -ĕre, **minuī, minūtum,** *lessen, diminish*

misceō -ēre, **miscuī, mixtum,** *mix*

misereor -ērī, **miseritus sum,** *pity*

miseret -ēre, **miseruit, ——,** *pity*

mittō -ĕre, **mīsī, missum,** *send*

mordeō -ēre, **momordī, morsum,** *bite*

morior -ī, **mortuus sum,** *die*

moveō -ēre, **mōvī, mōtum,** *move*

nancīscor -ī, **nānctus** *or* **nactus sum,** *obtain, find*

nāscor -ī, **nātus sum,** *be born*

neglegō -ĕre, **neglēxī, neglēctum,** *neglect*

niteo -ēre, **nituī, ——,** *shine*

nītor -ī, **nīsus** *or* **nīxus sum,** *lean, strive*

noceō -ēre, **nocuī, nocitum,** *harm*

nōlō -nōlle, **nōluī, ——,** *be unwilling*

nōscō -ĕre, **nōvī, nōtum,** *get to know*

nūbō -ĕre, **nūpsī, nūptum,** *marry*

obiciō -ĕre, **obiēcī, obiectum,** *throw in the way of*

oblīvīscor -ī, **oblītus sum,** *forget*

obsideō -ēre, **obsēdī, obsessum,** *besiege*

obsistō -ĕre, **obstitī, ——,** *stand in the way, resist*

obtineō -ēre, **obtinuī, obtentum,** *occupy, maintain*

occidō -ĕre, **occidī, occāsum,** *fall*

occīdō -ĕre, **occīdī, occīsum,** *kill*

occurrō -ĕre, **occurrī, occursum,** *meet*

ōdī -**ōdisse, ——,** *hate*

omittō -ĕre, **omīsī, omissum,** *leave out*

operiō -īre, **operuī, opertum,** *cover*

oportet -ēre, **oportuit, ——,** *ought*

opprimō -ĕre, **oppressī, oppressum,** *crush*

ōrdior -īrī, **ōrsus sum,** *begin*

orior -īrī, **ortus sum,** *arise*

ostendō -ĕre, **ostendī, ostentum,** *show*

pacīscor -ī, **pactus sum,** *make an agreement*

paenitet -ēre, **paenituit,** *repent of*

pandō -ĕre, **pandī, passum,** *spread out*

pangō -ĕre, **pepigī** *or* **pēgī, pāctum,** *fasten*

parcō -ĕre, **pepercī, parsum,** *spare*

pāreō -ēre, **pāruī, obtemperātum,** *obey*

pariō -ĕre, **peperī, partum** *or* **paritum,** *bring forth young, produce*

pāscō -ĕre, **pāvī, pāstum,** *feed*

patefaciō -ĕre, **patefēcī, patefactum,** *open*

pateō -ēre, **patuī, ——,** *be open*

patior -ī, **passus sum,** *suffer, allow*

paveō -ēre, **pāvī, ——,** *fear*
pellō -ĕre, **pepulī, pulsum,** *push, drive*
pendeō -ēre, **pependī, ——,** *hang*
pendō -ĕre, **pependī, pēnsum,** *weigh*
percellō -ĕre, **perculī, perculsum,** *strike*
percutiō -ĕre, **percussī, percussum,** *strike*
perdō -ĕre, **perdidī, perditum,** *destroy*
perficiō -ĕre, **perfēcī, perfectum,** *complete*
pergō -ĕre, **perrēxī, perrēctum,** *proceed*
perpetior -ī, **perpessus sum,** *endure*
perspiciō -ĕre, **perspexī, perspectum,** *observe*
pertineō -ēre, **pertinuī, ——,** *reach to, concern*
petō -ĕre, **petīvī, petītum,** *seek, make for, attack*
piget -ēre, **piguit, ——,** *it vexes*
plangō -ĕre, **planxī, planctum,** *beat, bewail*
pōnō -ĕre, **posuī, positum,** *place*
poscō -ĕre, **poposcī, ——,** *demand*
potior -īrī, **potītus sum,** *gain control of*
pōtō -āre, **pōtāvī, pōtātum** *or* **pōtum,** *drink*
praeficiō -ĕre, **praefēcī, praefectum,** *put in command of*
praestō -āre, **praestitī, praestatum,** *stand out, excel*
prehendō -ĕre, **prehendī, prehēnsum,** *seize*
premō -ĕre, **pressī, pressum,** *press*
prōdō -ĕre, **prōdidī, prōditum,** *betray*
proficīscor -ī, **profectus sum,** *set out*
prōgredior -ī, **prōgressus sum,** *advance*
prohibeō -ēre, **prohibuī, prohibitum,** *prevent*
prōiciō -ĕre, **prōiēcī, prōiectum,** *throw forward*
prōpellō -ĕre, **prōpulī, prōpulsum,** *drive forward*
prōspiciō -ĕre, **prōspexī, prōspectum,** *look forward*
pudet -ēre, **puduit, ——,** *be ashamed*
quaerō -ĕre, **quaesīvī, quaesītum,** *seek*
queror -ī, **questus sum,** *complain*
quiēscō -ĕre, **quiēvī, quiētum,** *rest*
rādō -ĕre, **rāsī, rāsum,** *scrape*
rapiō -ĕre, **rapuī, raptum,** *seize*

recipiō -ĕre, **recēpī, receptum,** *recover, welcome*
reddō -ĕre, **reddidī, redditum,** *give back*
redigō -ĕre, **redēgī, redāctum,** *drive back*
redimō -ĕre, **redēmī, redēmptum,** *buy back, ransom*
regredior -ī, **regressus sum,** *retreat*
relinquō -ĕre, **relīquī, relictum,** *leave behind*
reor -ērī, **ratus sum,** *think*
repellō -ĕre, **reppulī, repulsum,** *drive back*
reperiō -īre, **repperī, repertum,** *find out*
rēpō -ĕre, **rēpsī, rēptum,** *creep*
reprimō -ĕre, **repressī, repressum,** *hold back*
resistō -ĕre, **restitī, ——,** *resist*
respiciō -ĕre, **respexī, respectum,** *look back*
respondeō -ēre, **respondī, respōnsum,** *reply*
restituō -ĕre, **restituī, restitūtum,** *restore*
restō -āre, **restitī, ——,** *remain*
retineō -ēre, **retinuī, retentum,** *hold back*
revertor -ī, **revertī, reversum,** *turn back, return*
rīdeō -ēre, **rīsī, rīsum,** *laugh*
rumpō -ĕre, **rūpī, ruptum,** *burst*
ruō -ĕre, **ruī, rutum** *or* **ruitūrus,** *rush, fall*
saliō -īre, **saluī, ——,** *leap*
sanciō -īre, **sānxī, sānctum,** *decree, ratify*
scandō -ĕre, **scandī, scānsum,** *climb*
scindō -ĕre, **scidī, scissum,** *cut*
sciō -īre, **scīvī** *or* **sciī, scītum,** *know*
scrībō -ĕre, **scrīpsī, scriptum,** *write*
sculpō -ĕre, **sculpsī, sculptum,** *carve*
sēcernō -ĕre, **sēcrēvī, sēcrētum,** *set apart*
secō -āre, **secuī, sectum,** *cut*
sedeō -ēre, **sēdī, sessum,** *sit*
sentiō -īre, **sēnsī, sēnsum,** *feel, perceive*
sepeliō -īre, **sepelīvī, sepultum,** *bury*
sequor -ī, **secūtus sum,** *follow*
serō -ĕre, **sēvī, satum,** *sow*
serō -ĕre, **seruī, sertum,** *join*

serpō -ĕre, **serpsī, serptum,** *crawl*
sileō -ēre, **siluī, ——,** *be silent*
sinō -ĕre, **sīvī, situm,** *allow*
sistō -ĕre, **stitī, statum,** *set up*
soleō -ēre, **solitus sum,** *be accustomed to*
solvō -ĕre, **solvī, solūtum,** *loosen*
sonō -āre, **sonuī, sonitum,** *sound*
sortior -īrī, **sortītus sum,** *draw lots*
spargō -ĕre, **sparsī, sparsum,** *scatter*
spernō -ĕre, **sprēvī, sprētum,** *despise*
spondeō -ēre, **spopondī, spōnsum,** *promise, pledge oneself*
statuō -ĕre, **statuī, statūtum,** *decide, set up*
sternō -ĕre, **strāvī, strātum,** *lay low*
stō -āre, **stetī, stātum,** *stand*
strepō -ĕre, **strepuī, strepitum,** *make a noise*
stringō -ĕre, **strinxī, strictum,** *draw (a sword)*
struō -ĕre, **strūxī, strūctum,** *build, erect*
studeō -ēre, **studuī, ——,** *pay attention to, study*
suādeō -ēre, **suāsī, suāsum,** *advise*
subdō -ĕre, **subdidī, subditum,** *put beneath*
subigō -ĕre, **subēgī, subāctum,** *subdue*
succurrō -ĕre, **succurrī, succursum,** *help*
sūmō -ĕre, **sūmpsī, sūmptum,** *take up*
surgō -ĕre, **surrēxī, surrēctum,** *get up*
suscipiō -ĕre, **suscēpī, susceptum,** *undertake*
sustineō -ēre, **sustinuī, sustentum,** *withstand*
taedet -ēre, **taeduit** *or* **pertaesum est,** *it tires*
tangō -ĕre, **tetigī, tāctum,** *touch*
tegō -ĕre, **tēxī, tēctum,** *cover, protect*
tendō -ĕre, **tetendī, tentum** *or* **tēnsum,** *stretch*
teneō -ēre, **tenuī, tentum,** *hold*
terō -ĕre, **trīvī, trītum,** *rub*
texō -ĕre, **texuī, textum,** *weave*
timeō -ēre, **timuī, ——,** *fear*
tollō -ĕre, **sustulī, sublātum,** *lift, raise*
tondeō -ēre, **totondī, tōnsum,** *shear*

tonō -āre, **tonuī, tonitum,** *thunder*
torqueō -ēre, **torsī, tortum,** *twist*
torreō -ēre, **torruī, tostum,** *parch*
trādō -ĕre, **trādidī, trāditum,** *hand over*
trahō -ĕre, **trāxī, tractum,** *drag*
trāiciō -ĕre, **trāiēcī, trāiectum,** *take across*
tremō -ĕre, **tremuī, ——,** *tremble*
tribuō -ĕre, **tribuī, tribūtum,** *assign, distribute*
trūdō -ĕre, **trūsī, trūsum,** *thrust*
tueor -ērī, **tuitus sum,** *look at, protect*
tundō -ĕre, **tutudī, {tūnsum / tūsum},** *beat, bruise*
ulcīscor -ī, **ultus sum,** *avenge*
urgeō -ēre, **ursī, ——,** *urge, press hard*
urō -ĕre, **ussī, ustum,** *burn*
ūtor -ī, **ūsus sum,** *use*
vādō -ĕre, **——,** *go, walk*
vehō -ĕre, **vēxī, vectum,** *carry*
vellō -ĕre, **vellī, vulsum,** *pull*
vendō -ĕre, **vendidī, venditum,** *sell*
vēneō -īre, **vēniī, ——,** *be on sale, be sold*
veniō -īre, **vēnī, ventum,** *come*
vertō -ĕre, **vertī, versum,** *turn*
vēscor -ī, **——,** *eat, feed on*
vetō -āre, **vetuī, vetitum,** *forbid*
videō -ēre, **vīdī, vīsum,** *see*
vigeō -ēre, **viguī, ——,** *flourish*
vinciō -īre, **vinxī, vinctum,** *bind*
vincō -ĕre, **vīcī, victum,** *conquer*
vīsō -ĕre, **vīsī, ——,** *visit*
vīvō -ĕre, **vīxī, vīctum,** *live*
volō -velle, **voluī, ——,** *be willing, wish*
volvō -ĕre, **volvī, volūtum,** *roll*
voveō -ēre, **vōvī, vōtum,** *vow*

Index of Grammar

REFERENCES ARE TO SECTIONS

Latin Index

REFERENCES ARE TO SECTIONS